A LENTEN JOURNEY

TRAVELS IN THE SPIRITUAL LIFE BASED ON THE GOSPEL OF MARK

• LARRY R. •
KALAJAINEN

UPPER ROOM BOOKS
NASHVILLE

A Lenten Journey

Scripture quotations not otherwise identified are from the Revised Standard Version Bible, copyright 1946, 1952, 1971 by the Division of Christian Education of the National Council of Churches of Christ in the USA and are used by permission.

Scripture quotations designated REB are from the Revised English Bible, © Oxford University Press and Cambridge University Press 1989, and are used by permission of Cambridge University Press.

Scripture quotations designated AT are the author's translation from the Greek.

Prayer on page 91 taken from *Acts of Devotion,* ed. by George Appleton and reproduced by kind permission of SPCK London.

Excerpts from *The Way of the Heart* by Henri J. M. Nouwen. Copyright © 1981 by Henri J. M. Nouwen. Reprinted by permission of Harper & Row, Publishers, Inc.

"This World Is Not My Home" by Albert E. Brumley. © Copyright arrangement by Albert E. Brumley. Albert E. Brumley & Sons/SESAC. All rights reserved. Used by permission of Integrated Copyright Management Group, Inc.

Excerpt from *A Service of Word and Table 1,* © 1972, 1980, 1985, 1989 The United Methodist Publishing House. Used by permission.

"Soul of Christ" from *Modern Spiritual Exercises* by David L. Fleming. © 1983 by The Institute of Jesuit Sources. Used by permission of the Institute.

Cover Design: Jim Bateman
Cover Transparency: H. Armstrong Roberts, Inc.
Book Design: Jim Bateman
First Printing: November 1990 (10)
Second Printing: March 1992 (5)
Third Printing: October 1994 (3)
Library of Congress Catalog Card Number: 90-70324
ISBN: 0-8358-0616-2

Printed in the United States of America

For Carol,
who has graciously journeyed with me
these twenty-one years,
making my own journey so much richer

CONTENTS

INTRODUCTION

A. W. Tozer once preached a sermon entitled "Faith Is a Journey, Not a Destination."[1] Perhaps he took that title from the biblical metaphor which likens the people of God to "refugees" or "temporary residents." The writer of the Epistle to the Hebrews, after calling the roll of the heroes and heroines of faith, says, "These all died in faith, not having received what was promised, but having seen it and greeted it from afar, and having acknowledged that they were strangers and refugees (temporary residents) on the earth" (Heb. 11:13, AT). An old gospel song expressed the same truth:

> This world is not my home, I'm just a-passin' through;
> My treasures are laid up somewhere beyond the blue.
> The angels beckon me from heaven's open door,
> and I can't feel at home in this world anymore.

Though the thought expressed in the song has sometimes been used as an excuse to escape from responsible and active involvement in *this* world, it need not be so used. It also expresses the truth that the life of Christian discipleship is a life that is constantly on the move toward the kingdom of God. Growth, development, change, and movement belong to its very essence. Our goal is not this world, as it is now, but the new world that God is bringing into being through Jesus Christ.

Yet so many of us get hung up along the way. Sometimes when we reach a plateau in our spiritual development, we stop to build a house—or even a church! As a pastor, I often see Christians who have difficulty moving beyond a primary Sunday school level of faith development and who seem content to remain at that level for many years.

Richard J. Foster, in his book *Celebration of Discipline,* says, "Superficiality is the curse of our age. The doctrine of instant satisfaction is a primary spiritual problem. The desperate need today is not for a greater number of intelligent people, or gifted people, but for deep people."[2]

The seeming willingness of many Christians to remain at a comfortable, complacent level of spiritual development reminds me of the story of some frogs whose pond began to dry up during a long drought. Day by day, the pond grew smaller as the water evaporated. What water remained became stagnant. Eventually, the frog leader called all the frogs together and proposed that they begin a cross-country journey to find a new pond with more water in it. They agreed that they were badly in need of fresh water, so they accepted his proposal.

Early the next morning, they set out on their journey. As the day wore on, they became tired and overheated. Just when they thought they could go on no longer, they came to a road that was deeply rutted by the tires of passing trucks. It had rained the night before, and some of the ruts had fresh rainwater in them. The frogs joyfully splashed and played, refreshing themselves and resting. But before long, the leader gave the signal for the journey to continue. All of the frogs hopped out of the ruts and gathered together—all except one. This particular frog was having trouble getting out of his rut. It was an extremely deep rut, and though he gave a couple of good leaps, he didn't quite make it over the edge. The others gathered round and shouted encouragement to him, so he tried again, but with less enthusiasm. His memories of the heat and dryness and hard work of the journey were stronger than his desire to find a new pond. Besides, the rut had plenty of water in it and would collect more at the next rainfall. So he told his fellow frogs that he was content to remain behind and establish his new home in the rut. They pleaded with him, but to no avail. They could go; he would stay. With some sadness, the rest of the frogs continued on their journey. But they had not gone far when they looked around and saw their friend hopping furiously along behind them, trying desperately to catch up. They stopped and waited, and when he finally came to where they were, they asked him, "How did you manage to get out of your rut?"

"A big truck came along, and I had to get out," he replied.

On our own spiritual journeys, we often find comfortable ruts in which to dwell, and sometimes we are content to remain there. But if we try to stay there too long, the Holy Spirit comes along, prods us to get up, to leave our comfortable ruts, and to move on to deeper depths and higher heights of the spiritual life. Perhaps the nudging of the Spirit is not quite as irresistible or forceful as a speeding truck, but the Spirit does inspire within us a sense of holy discontent with our rut that can be a powerful incentive to move on. I'm convinced that many who are hearing that divine calling to continue the journey of faith lack the concrete knowledge of how to go about it. Some may have the vague feeling that more Bible reading or study and prayer have something to do with it, but they need specific help in discovering just what to do in those areas.

This course of spiritual exercises and meditations is an attempt to provide such help. It is certainly nothing like a complete manual for spiritual growth. It makes no attempt to be comprehensive. At best, it is an attempt to provide a starting point for the spiritual pilgrimage.

The course is structured in such a way as to address various aspects of spiritual life and growth as they have been passed down to us from both Western and Eastern traditions of Christian spirituality. Our heritage is a very rich one, and a recovery of that heritage will be a significant factor in a renewal of genuine Christian spirituality in our time. *Lectio Divina* (Divine Reading) was a development of the Middle Ages as a way leading to inner prayer. In this process, fathers and mothers of the faith often spoke of the spiritual disciplines of reading and living with the scriptures as consisting of four components: *lectio, meditatio, oratio,* and *contemplatio* (reading, meditation, prayer, and contemplation).

Lectio (Reading)

Lectio, or reading, means primarily the reading and study of the scriptures, although it has a much broader meaning than that. It includes reading of other spiritual writings, as well as the "reading" of God's revelation in creation, in history, and in the inner world of the spirit. Since, however, the scriptures are the Christian's primary source of coming into contact with God's revelation in human history, the emphasis is given to that particular kind of reading. Little spiritual progress can be realized apart from an engagement with the scriptures at a deep and personal level.

Central to the exercises in *A Lenten Journey* is the reading and praying of the Gospel of Mark. This is not an academic Bible study, however. We will not be concentrating on the historical settings, the critical problems, or the principles of interpretation of the Gospel. Rather, we shall be seeking to *pray* the Gospel, that is, to read it meditatively and prayerfully, seeking to allow the Lord's voice to speak to us through the words of the text. In the stories Mark tells us about Jesus and his disciples, we want to see the Risen Lord and hear his word to us.

Why the Gospel of Mark? Several reasons present themselves. One is simply its length, since it can be read in manageable portions during the six weeks of Lent. Another is the fact that Mark has structured his Gospel in such a way as to emphasize the journeys of Jesus and his disciples. Where they go is of some significance to Mark. For instance, most of the stories Mark tells us of Jesus' public ministry—his teachings, healing, and miracles of power—are set in Galilee, specifically in the vicinity of the Sea of Galilee. Throughout the first seven or eight chapters, we see Jesus crossing and re-crossing the sea, traveling from town to town.

In the middle of the Gospel, the action builds up to a dramatic event in Caesarea Philippi, and this becomes a turning point. From this point on, the spotlight of the writer is turned away from Jesus' ministry to the crowds and onto his ministry to his own disciples. Gradually, the action shifts from Galilee to Jerusalem. There are a number of stories and events which take place on the road to Jerusalem, and these are of great significance in understanding Mark's thinking about the meaning of discipleship. Finally, Jerusalem itself becomes the center of the action. Jesus' triumphal entry; his radical action in the Temple; his last meal with his disciples; his agony in Gethsemane; and his betrayal, arrest, trial, and execution—all happen in Jerusalem. At the end of the Gospel, in Mark's account of Jesus' resurrection, the women at the tomb (and perhaps the readers of the Gospel?) are sent back to Galilee, where it all began. So Mark is a gospel where journey is a key element; therefore it may lend itself to our attempts to follow Jesus on our own journeys of faith and discipleship.

Meditatio (Meditation)

Meditatio, or meditation, in the classical Christian tradition, meant the reception and repetition of a scripture text, often of a *word* (a single word or a whole phrase or sentence) which one received from scripture or, sometimes, received from one's spiritual father or mother. The interior repetition of this word or sentence would lead to the permanent shaping or forming of one's internal spiritual state and awareness of God. So in this course, suggestions for meditation using some classical "words" (single phrases or brief prayer petitions) will be given. Meditational formulas (mantras) possess no magical qualities in and of themselves. They are merely aids to centering one's attention and eliminating distractions. The ancient spiritual masters had a beautiful phrase for this centering; they called it "descending with the mind into the heart," of which we are reminded by the Russian mystic Theophan the Recluse. Anyone who has ever made a serious attempt to pray knows how the mind can be a source of distraction. Sometimes the harder one tries to focus on God, the more stray thoughts, memories, daydreams, and obsessions intrude. This inner noise prevents us from being in touch with our deepest selves. Since there is no inner stillness where all our being is focused, we have difficulty hearing the "still small voice" of the Spirit of God speaking from the deep center of our being. Centering, or centering down as it is sometimes referred to, means bringing our noisy inner self into focus, so that our attention is concentrated and our inner ear tuned to God. Meditational formulas, or mantras, can help in holding one's inner attention on God.

Oratio (Prayer)

Oratio, or prayer, is the response awakened by reading and meditation. Our reception of God's revelation draws us ever deeper into the new reality in which awareness of God creates and evokes—a response of gratitude, love, worship, and praise. Prayer is relationship, our reaching out in love to God and our reception of love from God. We sometimes take a too narrow view of prayer as only our speaking to God. But when we view prayer as any movement of the soul which deepens our relationship with God, we can greatly enrich our understanding and practice of prayer. Everything in our lives can be brought into God's presence, just as we bring our total selves into a relationship with a spouse or an intimate friend. Loving silences, arguments, questions, doubts, angers, adoring thoughts, quiet reflections, and joyous exclamations are all movements of the soul toward God—and this is prayer.

Prayer has both private and public dimensions, and neither can be omitted if prayer is to be genuine. Christian discipleship is deeply personal but never private. To be a disciple means to be in community. Public prayer, or the prayer of the community of faith expressed in the liturgy, provides the basis upon which the prayer of the individual must build. So both individual and corporate aspects of prayer will be addressed in this course.

Contemplatio (Contemplation)

The work of God in the soul is a living, growing reality. At times, that movement of God in the soul becomes so real to us that a word or an emotion or an act is inadequate to express it. Our whole personality, our whole being is suffused with love for God and reaches out toward God, wordlessly and even without conscious thought, until we are totally present to God and God to us.

This is *contemplatio* or contemplation. It is a gift, a special grace, given to those who have opened themselves to God by reading, meditation, and prayer. All Christians may experience this grace of contemplation; not all necessarily will, especially those who are beginners on the journey. And yet, I don't want to make this seem a grace attainable only by the spiritual elite. It is a gift of God, and God gives it where there is readiness. So contemplation, or the vision of God in the soul, will be that toward which we will move, with the awareness that it is not striving which grants this contemplative vision but God's mercy and grace.

Obviously, each of us is unique. No single method of prayer, of scriptural reflection, of exercise of spiritual discipline is appropriate to everyone. Different personality types and temperaments will find different forms or techniques of prayer most meaningful.[3] With that in mind, I have adopted an approach that offers a number of different techniques and borrows from the various schools of Christian spirituality. I do not think that every person will find every suggestion helpful. If, after trying a particular technique or suggestion, you do not find it meaningful, feel free to discard it, at least for the time being. (You may arrive at a point in your own journey where it will become meaningful.)

You will notice some other characteristics of the structure. One is the encouragement to use and memorize certain prayers which come to us from the distant past. One of the reasons these prayers have survived the centuries is that Christians in all ages have found them deeply meaningful. Some of them, like "Soul of Christ," were designed for personal use; others such as the *"Te Deum"* are part of the liturgy or public prayer of the church. It is my firm conviction that one of our deepest needs is to "think Christianly"; that is, to be able to react out of our Christian faith in every situation. The possession of such spiritual treasures as these prayers, embedded in our memories, can greatly help us make progress in having the mind of Christ (see Philippians 2:5).

The use of the Lord's Prayer each day also contributes to this process of learning to "think Christianly." Constant repetition of any word or action forms us. We are shaped by the things we say, hear, or do regularly. This model of prayer which our Lord gave us, repeated frequently, will become a permanent part of our own personal spiritual identity.

My hope is that you will use these prayers so regularly and frequently that even when you are occupied with other matters, you will hear their phrases and cadences echoing in your inner ear. When that happens, you will be approaching something of what the Apostle Paul meant when he said, "Pray without ceasing" (Rom. 5:17). Your whole being will be tuned in to God. That is the end and goal of any spiritual discipline. Abraham Joshua Heschel has said it well:

> The purpose of prayer is to be brought to [God's] attention, to be listened to, to be understood by [God]; not to know [God], but to *be known to* [God] . . . To live "in the light of [God's] countenance," to become a thought of God—this is the true career of [a human being].[4]

My prayer is that as we enter upon this Lenten journey together, we will all be drawn closer to the One who has charted the path in this world of the Spirit, the "pioneer and the perfecter of our faith" (Heb. 12:21). As we are drawn closer to Christ, we will inevitably be drawn closer to one another, and out of our life together we will find ourselves sent forth in mission and service to the world around us.

Bon Voyage!

HOW TO USE THIS COURSE

When any program or procedure is presented to us, our natural tendency is to try to follow it as precisely as possible. If you conscientiously attempt to follow every suggestion in the lessons ahead or meditate on each reflection question every day, you will find yourself overloaded in a very short time. There is a great deal of material here, but you must pick and choose those procedures, methods, suggestions, and reflections each day which mean the most to you and which allow you to move deeper into prayer. *Not everything every day is for everyone.* If the use of mantra-like meditation formulas do not do anything for you, forget them and pass on to something that does meet your needs and suit your personality. However, don't pass over something just because it's unfamiliar. Growth always means moving beyond the tried and true. Likewise, if trying to "read" scripture by imagining yourself in the story doesn't work for you, reflect on the passage in a way that does.

Keep in mind that if you miss one day, you do not have to catch up the next day by doing two lessons. That will lead to certain frustration.

But do read and reflect on the scripture passage each day, since an engagement with the scriptures is fundamental to Christian prayer. Equally fundamental is a balance between prayer and action, or between the inward journey and the outward journey. Concentration on one to the exclusion of the other will result either in a self-centered narcissism or sterile activism. So try to keep your balance. As the Lenten days progress, the suggested outward journey becomes more outwardly oriented.

In addition, some of the "Journey Outward" sections suggest an activity for the day. If you read the meditation and exercises at the end of your day instead of at the beginning, simply carry out the suggestions the following day.

Above all, don't let this course become either a crushing burden or another source of guilt. Prayer ought to be as natural as breathing and as satisfying as food to a hungry person. Simply setting aside a regular time for prayer will be a new task for some. But the point of any discipline is that in time the action becomes automatic and part of our characters. We become formed by it.

As a note of explanation: While many Protestants place little importance on reference to certain persons as "saints," I have chosen to keep the designation *Saint (St.)* with the names of some of the great teachers and pray-ers of the past. The title has become deeply embedded in the historical church tradition, and one encounters it frequently in many sources. The title denotes these individuals as exemplary Christians and recognizes their gifts to the church universal. I like what C. S. Lewis said in *Letters to Malcolm,* that while Christians may disagree about the practice of praying *to* the saints, we all agree that we pray *with* the saints.

The Use of a Journal

Most of the spiritual giants have written extensively or kept a personal journal in which they recorded thoughts, reflections on scripture, feelings, confessions, prayers, notes on their work, records of encounters. St. Augustine, St. Teresa of Avila, John Wesley, David Brainerd, Simone Weil, and Dag Hammarskjöld are among the more illustrious spiritual writers or journal-keepers.

Those who choose to keep a journal will find doing so an enormously helpful tool to aid their growth in the spiritual life. Ronald Klug in his book *How to Keep a Spiritual Journal* lists ten reasons for using a journal: growth in self-understanding, aiding the devotional life, guidance and decision-making, making sense and order of life, releasing emotions and gaining perspective, greater awareness of daily life, self-expression and creativity, clarifying beliefs, setting goals and managing time, and working through problems.[5] More reasons could be added to this list. Although keeping a journal is optional to completing this Lenten study, I think you would find it an invaluable aid in making progress in your spiritual journey. Spaces are provided in each day's exercises for you to record your reflections.

What should you write in your journal? Anything and everything. Your personal reflections on the scripture reading of the day; a prayer that you compose; your recollection of your dreams; your feelings about people, situations, and events; quotations from readings; poems. Everything is grist for the journal. Entries can be as lengthy or as brief as you choose to make them. The important thing is that your journal is your personal and *private* sounding board. If you don't feel like writing some days, then don't. If you feel like writing a major epistle to yourself or to God, then write as much as you like. You will gain a great deal of insight into yourself by writing and by periodically looking back over what you have written weeks and months and even years before. Your spiritual pilgrimage will have left a clear path.

JOURNEY INTO THE WILDERNESS
WILD BEASTS AND ANGELS

Solitude is the furnace of transformation. Without solitude we remain victims of our society and continue to be entangled in the illusions of the false self. . . . Solitude is the place of the great struggle and the great encounter—the struggle against the compulsions of the false self, and the encounter with the loving God who offers [the Divine Self] as the substance of the new self.
—Henri J. M. Nouwen, *The Way of the Heart* [6]

Preparation

Find a quiet place and a quiet time. Sit in a comfortable position. Take a moment to remind yourself why you are here and what a privilege is yours to make yourself present to God. Use the following prayer, "Soul of Christ," to recollect yourself.

Jesus, may all that is you flow into me.
May your body and blood be my food and drink.
May your passion and death be my strength and life.
Jesus, with you by my side enough has been given.
May the shelter I seek be the shadow of your cross.
Let me not run from the love which you offer,
But hold me safe from the forces of evil.
On each of my dyings shed your light and your love.
Keep calling to me until that day comes,
When, with your saints, I may praise you forever. Amen. [7]

Scripture: Read Mark 1:1-13.

The "beginning of the gospel," as Mark styles it, takes place in the wilderness of Judea, where a rather colorful character named John is preaching "a baptism of repentance for the forgiveness of sins" (verse 4). Jesus comes into this wilderness and is himself baptized by John. Clues to Mark's emphasis are John's proclamation in verse 8 that the one coming after him will baptize "in the Holy Spirit" (verse 8, AT) and verses 9-11, where at Jesus' baptism the Holy Spirit is given to him accompanied by a heavenly voice announcing divine approval. This one who receives the Spirit of God will also "baptize" others in the Spirit.

Immediately, however (notice how frequently Mark uses the word *immediately*), the Holy Spirit "drives" Jesus into the "wilderness." Pay particular attention to Mark's description of that wilderness experience.

JOURNEY INWARD
Hearing and Seeing

Reflect for a few moments on the meaning of *wilderness* for Mark. It is the place where people go to express their repentance. It is the place of Jesus' anointing and commission. It is the place where Jesus is tested for forty days. It is in the wilderness that Jesus is ministered to by angels.

Forty is an important symbolic number. In the story of Noah, the rain lasted forty days and forty nights, Moses was forty days on Mt. Sinai, Israel wandered forty years in the wilderness, Elijah was sustained forty days in the wilderness when he fled from Ahab, and Jonah announced that Nineveh would be overthrown in forty days. The church's observance of the forty days of Lent (Sundays excepted, as they are feast days in Lent) is a recognition of the importance of the number *forty* in scripture and of the wilderness experience—both of Jesus and of those who are called to follow him.

What wilderness experiences have you known in your life? When have you been aware you were being tested for some future work? Have you felt the sense of loneliness that the word *wilderness* conjures up? Describe that loneliness. You may use the space below to write a few sentences exploring your own wilderness experiences.

In your own wilderness times, are you more aware of the "wild beasts" or the "angels"? Is it possible that the wilderness can be both a place where we face testing, fear, and loneliness, and a place where we are strengthened and renewed for mission? If you can, describe a time when you were more aware of the "wild beasts" and a time when you were more aware of "angels."

Reflect for a few moments on the beginning quotation from *The Way of the Heart*. What connection do you see between these thoughts on solitude and the wilderness of temptation for Jesus? For you in your own wilderness experience? You may find it helpful to write your reflections to preserve a record of your insights.

As you read the Gospel of Mark, notice other places where Jesus withdraws to the wilderness or "a lonely place" and what happens at those times.

Ash Wednesday is a time for repentance. Look within yourself and allow God's spirit to point out to you those habits, attitudes, and behaviors which may be blocking you from a deeper walk with God. You may wish to write these down. Writing can help us to be truthful with ourselves. When you have named those roadblocks which hinder your journey, ask for and receive God's forgiveness.

Meditation and Prayer

Out of the teachings of Abba Isaac, a desert father of the fourth century, comes a meditation formula for "descending with the mind into the heart," a common expression for withdrawing from distractions and centering oneself in God's presence. Begin with this verse from Psalm 40:13 (early translation): "O God, come to my assistance; O Lord, make haste to help me." In *Centering Prayer* Basil Pennington says of this verse,

> Rightly has this verse been selected from the whole Bible to serve this purpose. It suits every mood and temper of human nature, every temptation, every circumstance. It contains an invocation of God, a humble confession of faith, a reverent watchfulness, a meditation on human frailty, an act of confidence in God's response, an assurance of ever-present support. The [person] who continually invokes God as his [or her] protector is aware that God is ever at hand.[8]

Spend two or three minutes repeating this prayer silently. While praying, breathe deeply and rhythmically, perhaps saying the first phrase of the prayer while inhaling and the second phrase while exhaling. Remember, the point is to focus attention not on the prayer itself or on your bodily state but on God.

While you are aware of being in God's presence, lift up to God your concerns for others. You may name these persons or simply imagine them being in the Divine Presence, where God's perfect knowledge of them meets their needs.

Conclude the time of prayer by slowly and thoughtfully praying the Lord's Prayer.

JOURNEY OUTWARD

As you go about your daily routine, look around you and consciously attempt to "read" God's revelation in the world around you. Also, use the prayer "O God, come to my assistance; O Lord, make haste to help me" at frequent intervals throughout the day—while driving or while preparing dinner, for example. The point of this exercise is to increase your attentiveness to God amid the ordinary activities of everyday life.

Let people and events of your day call you to lift them into the presence of God as you seek to be attentive to that presence.

JOURNEY IN GALILEE
REPENTANCE

Preparation

Begin your time of prayer by slowly and thoughtfully repeating the prayer "Soul of Christ" (see page 15).

Scripture: Read Mark 1:14-20.

Verse 14 sets the stage for Jesus' public ministry in this Gospel. In Galilee Jesus directs his attention to the crowds. His characteristic activity in Galilee consists of calling, preaching, teaching, healing, exorcism, and acts of power. Galilee, then, is the place where people are to see and hear Jesus and come to some point of decision or response. In verse 15 Mark summarizes the whole of Jesus' ministry— "preaching the gospel of God," which, for Mark, consists of the call to repentance and the proclamation of the kingdom of God. The calling of Peter, James, and John is his first act; and Mark's placement of it immediately after his summary of Jesus' message lets us know that such a message always results in a calling out of a community of disciples.

JOURNEY INWARD
Hearing and Seeing

Repentance means more than being sorry for our sins. It means literally "to turn around." So repentance is more than a one-time thing; it is a way of life which continually orients itself away from the world and toward God. What will it mean for you to heed Jesus' call to repentance? What will you have to turn away from?

How is repentance illustrated in the lives of the three disciples Jesus called? Has your response to Christ been as immediate? Peter left behind his fishing nets (livelihood). James and John left not only their nets but their father as well (family expectations). What are the equivalents of fishing nets and fathers in your life?

Meditation and Prayer

Spend two or three minutes centering by using Abba Isaac's prayer "O God, come to my assistance; O Lord, make haste to help me."

Listen for Christ's call to you. Open yourself as fully as possible to the Spirit's inner promptings. As you become aware of attachments or obstacles in your life which are preventing you from wholeheartedly following Christ, surrender them to the Lord as far as you are able.

Pray for grace to repent of an old grudge or resentment to which you have been clinging. Ask for healing of that wound in your life and pray for blessing on the one against whom you've had the grudge.

Conclude with the Lord's Prayer.

JOURNEY OUTWARD

Again, practice the habit of paying attention to God throughout the day. Use the prayer formula of Abba Isaac to aid you. Begin memorizing the prayer "Soul of Christ" (see page 15).

Think of one thing you need to do but have been putting off and do it.

JOURNEY IN GALILEE
FORGIVENESS

Preparation

Remind yourself that you are bringing yourself to meet God, the God who loves you and wishes to reveal the Divine Self to you. Pray the "Soul of Christ" (see page 15).

Scripture: Read Mark 2:1-12.

Mark takes the story of a healing and turns it into a story emphasizing the authority of Jesus. In response to the faith of the friends (verse 5), Jesus announces that the sick man's sins are forgiven. This leads to the charge by the onlookers that he has committed blasphemy by usurping God's prerogatives. Jesus counters this charge by healing the man's paralysis.

JOURNEY INWARD
Hearing and Seeing

Why does Jesus address himself to the man's inner spiritual needs before healing his physical infirmity? What does this suggest about possible connections between the spiritual and physical condition of human beings? What is the connection between faith and forgiveness (verse 5)?

In your imagination, put yourself in the place of the paralyzed man. What sins are paralyzing you? Who are the friends whose faith can help carry you into the forgiving and healing presence of Christ? Imagine Christ putting his hand on your shoulder and saying, "Rise, take up your pallet and walk." What risk is there for you in obeying this authoritative word?

Meditation and Prayer

You might try using music as a means to help you center down, or recollect yourself. Listen to music that quiets the noise of the distractions and busyness of your day. Or sing a favorite hymn which leads your mind and heart to God.

If music is not useful in leading you into prayer, spend about 3 to 5 minutes in complete silence instead. If you are troubled by distracting thoughts, pray: "O God, come to my assistance; O Lord, make haste to help me." Repeat it slowly while you breathe rhythmically. Say the first phrase while breathing in, holding the breath for a few seconds; then exhale while saying the last phrase.

Intercede for others by imagining them in the story of the healing of the paralytic. In your mind's eye, see them being forgiven and healed by Jesus.

Finish your time of prayer with the Lord's Prayer.

JOURNEY OUTWARD

Lent is traditionally observed by some concrete act of self-denial. This is undertaken as a means of self-discipline and sacrificial identification with the sufferings of Christ. Often Christians have fasted on Fridays during Lent. If you are so minded, fast one meal today or sometime this week. Don't eat extra heavily at the meal before or after. Use your fasting time to pray for the needs of those in our world who are hungry. (CAUTION: Because of medical disorders or other conditions, some persons probably should not fast from food. If you cannot fast from food, try fasting from speech for a predetermined period, or perhaps fasting from some other legitimate pleasure which you can offer up as a sacrifice.) If you do choose to fast, you may want to plan to fast each Friday during Lent.

JOURNEY IN GALILEE
OLD WINESKINS, NEW WINE

Preparation

Pray the prayer "Soul of Christ" (see page 15) while sitting comfortably in a quiet place. Reflect briefly on each phrase as you say it.

Scripture: Read Mark 2:18–3:6.

In these stories, we see Jesus beginning to run into questioning and opposition. His association with known sinners, his failure (and that of his disciples) to observe the ritual laws of fasting, and his healing on the sabbath provoke a strong reaction, especially from religious people. This opposition builds from polite questioning to a hard and angry plot to destroy him. So threatening is Jesus that even traditional enemies like the Pharisees and the Herodians join forces against him.

JOURNEY INWARD
Hearing and Seeing

What are some "old wineskins" in your life which may not be able to hold the "new wine" Jesus represents? Think first about personal habits. Then move on to your behavior in relationship to other people—your business ethics, your prejudices, your defense mechanisms. Write your thoughts in the space provided or in your journal. Somehow, it is hard to deceive oneself in writing. The self-deception stands out immediately when we read what we have written. Throw away the old wineskin in your life by taking some definite action. Deliberately attempt to become a new wineskin at that point.

Do you find Jesus and his demand for repentance, for new wineskins, threatening? If so, why? Are you the kind of person who cares more about playing by the rules than about being sensitive to people's needs? Are there things about which you have a case of "hardness of heart"? Name some of those things.

Meditation and Prayer

From the Eastern Christian tradition comes another prayer which many have used for centuries as a means of holding themselves at attention before God. It is often referred to as the Jesus Prayer. It functions much the same as Abba Isaac's prayer formula. It simply says, "Lord Jesus Christ, Son of the living God, have mercy on me, a sinner." Use it today as a means of becoming inwardly still and free from distractions. Spend time in silence using the Jesus Prayer as you breathe deeply and rhythmically. Try saying the first part, "Lord, Jesus Christ, Son of the living God," as you inhale and the final part, "have mercy on me, a sinner," as you exhale.

Tell God the old wineskins in your life. Open yourself to God's new wine.

Pray for the needs of others for whom you are concerned, especially those whose needs are brought on by behavior of which you do not approve. Ask God to give you love in place of disapproving and judgmental attitudes.

Close your prayer time with the Lord's Prayer.

JOURNEY OUTWARD

Repeat the Jesus Prayer frequently throughout the day. This frequent repetition is training your mind and spirit to be attentive to God. If after some experimentation you find you prefer the Abba Isaac prayer formula, use it instead. Or choose a verse from the Psalms or a sentence prayer of your own making. The point is, to hold yourself open to God.

Pray for three people you encounter today.

THE LORD'S DAY

JOURNEY IN GALILEE
THE PRESENCE OF EVIL AND THE POWER OF THE COMMUNITY

Preparation

Pray the "Soul of Christ" prayer (see page 15) from memory as much as possible.

Scripture: Read Mark 3:7-19a.

Numerous times throughout the Galilean portion of the Gospel, Mark has Jesus going "to the sea," "by the sea," "along the sea," or even "on the sea." Each time, the sea is the setting for Jesus' characteristic activity of teaching the crowds (see 2:13-14; 3:7; 4:1-2; 5:21). The sea is also the place where he calls disciples.

Mark includes here the tradition of Jesus calling the twelve disciples. Mark's phrasing is significant: "He appointed twelve *to be with him*" (verse 15, italics added). *Being with Jesus* means that these disciples are "sent out to preach" and "have authority to cast out demons," both of which are activities characteristic of Jesus' ministry, according to Mark. In other words, the disciples, in community, become extensions of Jesus himself.

JOURNEY INWARD
Hearing and Seeing

Why do you think the Pharisees (see 3:1-6) are unable to recognize the divine authority in Jesus when he healed a man on the Sabbath, but the demons do recognize his authority (3:7-12)?

In Jesus' time and culture, demons or evil spirits were accepted as a reality. Many persons in our time find it difficult to believe in actual supernatural beings who are the emissaries of Satan; they prefer to speak of "forces of evil" and to locate these "demons" in human attitudes and in oppressive political or economic or social structures. Don't get bogged down at this point. The question of the *nature* or *form* of demons is less important than the question of their influence on our lives. However we conceive of them, the powers of evil are real, and we are the targets of those powers. Look within yourself or at your circumstances for indications of the presence and power of evil. Where are you most vulnerable? Where do you feel evil approaching you most closely? It may be helpful to list those areas as a way of seeing them more clearly.

Reflect on Mark's insistence that disciples of Jesus are given authority over evil. Have you ever experienced that authority? In what way(s)?

Meditation and Prayer

Reflect throughout the day on the meaning of the community of disciples. Being part of the community goes along with being a follower of Jesus. Worship and prayer in community is an essential spiritual discipline. Resolve to accept this discipline and reflect on your habits of church attendance and participation in ministry. Do they manifest your understanding of the corporate nature of discipleship?

JOURNEY OUTWARD

Prayer is always deeply personal but never purely private. True prayer always involves community. Jesus himself called a community into being to "be with him." So today, go to church and pray in and with the community of believers of which you are a part. As you join in the corporate prayer of God's people, pay particular attention to the different forms of prayer used in the worship service—hymns, scriptures, sermon, intercessions, confessions, Eucharist, responses. Reflect on the purpose of each part of the service. If you are reading this in the evening, reflect on the morning's worship service you attended or on a worship experience from an earlier date.

JOURNEY IN GALILEE
UNBELIEF

Preparation

Today, use the *Te Deum* ("We Praise Thee") to prepare yourself for your time with God. This prayer is an ancient one from about the fourth century. It is a wonderful expression both of worship and of Christian doctrine. Throughout the next week, we will concentrate on various parts of it. Today, read the whole prayer slowly and thoughtfully. Let its words become yours.

We praise thee, O God; we acknowledge thee to be the Lord.
All the earth doth worship thee, the Father everlasting.
To thee all angels cry aloud; the heavens, and all the powers therein;
To thee, cherubim and seraphim continually do cry.
Holy, holy, holy, Lord God of hosts;
Heaven and earth are full of the majesty of thy glory.
The glorious company of the apostles praise thee.
The goodly fellowship of the prophets praise thee.
The noble army of martyrs praise thee.
The holy Church throughout all the world doth acknowledge thee;
The Father, of an infinite majesty; thine adorable, true, and only Son;
also the Holy Ghost, the Comforter.

Thou art the King of Glory, O Christ.
Thou art the everlasting Son of the Father.
When thou tookest upon thee to deliver man,
Thou didst humble thyself to be born of a virgin.
When thou hadst overcome the sharpness of death,
Thou didst open the kingdom of heaven to all believers.
Thou sittest at the right hand of God,
In the glory of the Father.
We believe that thou shalt come to be our judge.
We therefore pray thee, help thy servants,
Whom thou hast redeemed with thy precious blood.
Make them to be numbered with thy saints, in glory everlasting.

O Lord, save thy people, and bless thine heritage.
Govern them, and lift them up forever.
Day by day we magnify thee;
And we worship thy name ever, world without end.
Vouchsafe, O Lord, to keep us this day without sin.
O Lord, have mercy upon us, have mercy upon us.
O Lord, let thy mercy be upon us, as our trust is in thee.
O Lord, in thee have I trusted; let me never be confounded.

Scripture: Read Mark 3:19b-35.

In verse 21, the word translated *friends* more correctly means "relatives." Verses 19*b*-21 and 31-35 are all one story; verses 22-30 are another. Mark's technique of inserting one story into the middle of another is characteristic of his style. (Compare this with Mark 5:21-43.) This technique is used effectively to link the two stories so that they intensify one another. In this instance, Jesus' relatives, who think he's insane, and the "scribes who came down from Jerusalem" (that is, the religious establishment) have a similar response to Jesus—unbelief.

JOURNEY INWARD
Hearing and Seeing

In this context, what is the "eternal sin"? How can anyone see and hear Jesus in his journey through Galilee and conclude that he is "beside himself" (literally, "insane," verse 21) or "possessed by Beelzebul" (verse 22—Beelzebul was considered the head of the demon armies)? Reflect that it was not only the most religious people of the day who felt that way about Jesus but even his own family members. What does this tell us, perhaps, about the difficulty of depending on miraculous signs as healings and exorcisms for proof of God's activity? What does it tell us about the tendency for those closest to Jesus to fall into unbelief? Ask yourself, *When have I, either through indifference or actual resistance, lived or acted as though there were no God?*

Meditation and Prayer

Spend at least five minutes today in absolute silence, keeping yourself in peaceful attention to God. Use Abba Isaac's prayer formula (see page 17) or the Jesus Prayer (see page 23) to help if you need to block out distractions. If you find that five minutes seems like a long time, persevere. Only your inner noise and false self makes silence seem uncomfortable. In your silence, reach out in love with your spirit toward God. Don't *think* about God. Simply love God.

Conclude with the Lord's Prayer.

JOURNEY OUTWARD

Try to be conscious of ways in which you seem to be "possessed." What is it that dominates your thoughts, your behavior, your goals? Write your reflections here or in your journal. Be honest with yourself. Otherwise, you cannot be honest with others or with God.

As you meet other people today, try to become sensitive to what they are saying about themselves, not necessarily in words but in facial expressions, body language, tone of voice. Pray for their needs as far as you are able to become aware of these needs.

JOURNEY IN GALILEE
GOOD SOIL

Preparation

Concentrate on the first section of the *Te Deum* (see page 26). Pay attention to all the different ways God is praised in it. Reflect that the first duty of every Christian is to praise and worship God. Begin to memorize this first section by reading over and praying it several times.

Scripture: Read Mark 4:1-9, 14-20.

Chapter 4 is extremely important for understanding what Mark is trying to say in his Gospel. In it he offers some clues about how one reads and appropriates the Gospel, as well as how one "hears and sees" Jesus. The chapter contains two groups of materials: parables and material about parables. Today and tomorrow we will look at the parables themselves. Parables were probably the most characteristic form of the teaching of Jesus.

JOURNEY INWARD
Hearing and Seeing

Picture yourself as one of the soils upon which the seed falls in the parable of the sower. Which kind of soil are you? What evidence is there in your life that God's word has taken root? What evidence is there that you are bearing fruit? You may wish to write your reflections here.

Is there a sense in which each type of soil is characteristic of our lives at particular points along our journeys? When has your life been variously the hardened soil of the path, the rocky soil, the soil choked with thorns, and the good soil?

Meditation and Prayer

Again, spend time in silence. Use the Jesus Prayer (see page 23) or Abba Isaac's prayer formula (see page 17) to help you if you are distracted by wandering thoughts, inner turmoil, or noise. Apart from the use of the centering formulas, try not to form words, even silently. Concentrate on simply reaching out toward God in love with your spirit. You may find it helpful to form a mental image or picture of yourself sitting at Jesus' feet or walking with him along a beautiful country road or by the seaside. Just enjoy his presence in quietness. The value of silence is that it is the place of the meeting between yourself and God.

Pray for one specific situation or person with whom you're involved. Seek the Lord's guidance in knowing how to be sensitive to that person or situation and to be available for ministry.

Conclude your time with the Lord's Prayer.

JOURNEY OUTWARD

Try to identify "good soils" around you. Look for places and people where the Lord may be calling you to spread God's word and where the Lord has been preparing the soil to receive your witness.

As you read or watch a TV program today, pay attention to human situations which call for Christian compassion and mission. Pray about ways in which you and the Christian community of which you are a part can bring compassion and God's presence to bear in similar situations which confront you.

JOURNEY IN GALILEE
MYSTERIOUS GROWTH OF THE KINGDOM

Preparation

Focus today on the second section of the *Te Deum* (see page 26). As you pray these wonderful ascriptions of praise, pay attention to what you are saying. This section is really a creed, an affirmation of faith.

Scripture: Read Mark 4:26-32.

In some respects, these two parables form a counterpoint to the parable of the sower. In the latter, the human response to the message is emphasized in the descriptions of the various soils. Here, the emphasis is on the natural and mysterious growth of the kingdom apart from human effort. While the farmer sleeps, the seed grows. The mustard seed is of insignificant size, but its growth is all out of proportion to its size.

JOURNEY INWARD
Hearing and Seeing

One of the most common pitfalls in the spiritual life is the compulsive feeling that all growth or progress depends on our own efforts or willpower. (If I just were more disciplined, I could pray better. If I just could be more consistent, I know I would grow.) How do the two parables you read today speak to your own compulsions and perfectionisms?

Meditation and Prayer

Use centering prayer in silence for a time. When you are focused and the inner noise has gotten quieter, bring your compulsions into God's presence. Praise God for God's sovereignty and power, and ask for release from the inner need to perform perfectly. Consciously, as much as you are able, turn over these compulsions to Christ and begin to rest while the Lord does the work of producing growth in you.

Conclude with the Lord's Prayer.

JOURNEY OUTWARD

As you go through the day, try to be aware of actions that are motivated by a perfectionist inner drive and seek to rest in Christ.

Continue your research into a current issue or problem that interests you and demands to be addressed in faith. Pray about any issue or problem that particularly stays in your mind, asking what action you or your particular community of faith might take to address the need evident there.

JOURNEY IN GALILEE
SEEING WHAT WE HEAR

Preparation

Pray slowly and thoughtfully the third section of the *Te Deum* (see page 26). Reflect on the meaning of each of the petitions.

Scripture: Read Mark 4:10-13, 21-25, 33-34.

These verses are crucial to an understanding of Mark, yet difficult enough to have kept scholars busy for centuries. Verses 10-13 raise questions: What is the difference between "insiders" and "outsiders"? What is there about parables that conceals rather than reveals? What is the purpose of parables in Mark's view? Verses 21-25 seem to suggest that hidden things are meant to be revealed, and yet the disciples, who apparently are insiders, have to have private explanations of everything.

JOURNEY INWARD
Hearing and Seeing

What do verses 10-12 suggest to you about the act or process of hearing and seeing the "secret of the kingdom of God"? Is the proclamation of the kingdom always good news, or is it also a judgment for those whose spiritual hearing is impaired? When have you experienced or witnessed the deafness and blindness that comes from rejection of the truth in yourself or someone else?

Verse 24 contains a peculiar expression which, in a literal translation reads, "See what you hear" (AT). How does one "see" something that is "heard"? What does this say to you about the relationship between one's response to God and one's ability to understand and grasp reality or the truth? How do you see what you hear?

Meditation and Prayer

Begin your prayer time by meditating on that command of Jesus, "See what you hear." When you have begun to grasp that command, pray for healing for your own inner blindness and deafness to God's voice.

Conclude with the Lord's Prayer.

JOURNEY OUTWARD

As you go about today, try to be sensitive to all the different ways and media through which God's word comes to you. In other words, make a conscious effort to "see what you hear." At the end of the day, make a list of what you have seen / heard and the way that word came to you.

JOURNEY IN GALILEE
THE STORMS OF LIFE

Preparation

In the *Te Deum* there is a beautiful petition: "Vouchsafe, O Lord, to keep us this day without sin." Pray this petition for several minutes as a means of centering down.

Scripture: Read Mark 4:35-41.

The group of four miracle stories which begins here and concludes with 5:43 may have been linked in the tradition before Mark included them in his Gospel. As you move through them the next four days, think of them in relationship to each other as well as individually. Compare this story with Psalm 107:23-30.

JOURNEY INWARD
Hearing and Seeing

Think of the biggest "storm" you've ever gone through. Were you afraid? Why? Why does Jesus put the attitudes of fear and faith in opposition to each other? Is fear the same as unbelief? In the space below, name one or more of your fears that have crippled your faith during life's storms.

What is your answer to the question the disciples ask, "Who is this man?" Is it possible to be a disciple and still be asking that question? Why or why not?

Meditation and Prayer

Spend some time in silence, using whatever centering technique you find helpful, as long as it helps you center on God rather than on yourself. Let your soul go out in love to God. When names of people come into your mind, include them in the reaching out of your spirit to God in love.

Keep your journal near and write down anything you may feel the Lord is trying to say to you.

Conclude with the Lord's Prayer.

JOURNEY OUTWARD

If you have chosen to fast each Friday during Lent, fast at least one meal today. You may even want to fast one whole day. If you decide on a longer fast, be sure to drink plenty of water to prevent dehydration. Break your fast with fruit juices or liquids to begin with and then eat lightly. Remember that if you should not abstain from foods for medical reasons, you may fast in some other way, perhaps abstaining from conversation for a specified period.

While fasting itself is an inward discipline, there are things you can do while fasting to turn the focus onto the outward journey. While fasting, read a book or an article about world hunger. Let the hunger pangs you feel while fasting help you to identify partially with those whose hunger is not voluntary but a terrifying way of life. Reflect on your own ways of living that might be contributing to problems of world hunger. For example, does your diet reflect the beef-heavy American diet which demands so much grain for animal feed? (It takes eight pounds of grain to produce one pound of beef, while it takes only one pound of grain to produce one pound of chicken.)

Follow up on whatever you read or saw regarding a situation of human need. If you have ideas you want to bring to your faith community or a study or prayer group about ways in which the group or community might be involved, write them down.

JOURNEY IN GALILEE
ORDER OUT OF CHAOS

Preparation

Dwell on this petition from the *Te Deum:* "Day by day we magnify thee, and we worship thy name ever, world without end." Let your praise bring you into God's presence.

Scripture: Read Mark 5:1-20.

To a Jewish audience, the story of the demons entering a herd of pigs would have provided a touch of ironic humor. The hopelessness of the possessed man's condition is emphasized by Mark's description of previous attempts to help him. This heightens the drama and makes Jesus' intervention all that much more significant.

JOURNEY INWARD
Hearing and Seeing

Have you ever felt that your sins, your weaknesses, your liabilities, or your problems were so overwhelming that you could say, "My name is Legion, for we are many"? When? Reflect on how many solutions to the possessed man's problems had been tried and how all had failed. Do you have an "impossible" situation in your life? What does the authority of Jesus to drive out the Legion have to say to you?

Meditation and Prayer

The last petition in the *Te Deum* relates well to both the story of the stilling of the storm and this story. "Let me never be confounded" is perhaps one of the most meaningful and profound prayers we can pray. To understand something of its depth, we must first understand what it means. In the scriptures, God's creating and sustaining activity always tends toward order or harmony. The biblical word for this is *cosmos*. The antithesis of cosmos is chaos, or confusion, the force which opposes the order of creation. In the creation story of Genesis, we are told, "The Spirit of God hovered over the face of the chaos" (AT from the Hebrew). Then come the creative acts of God: "And God said, 'Let there be. . . .'" Out of chaos comes cosmos—divinely given order or harmony. So the prayer "Let me never be confounded" is a plea that my life will not dissolve back into chaos or confusion but will know and manifest the harmony of God's creative and sustaining work.

Spend some time in silence simply repeating that one petition. Allow the Holy Spirit to hover over your personal chaos and bring order to it.

As the Lord leads, pray for others who are in chaotic situations.

Conclude with the Lord's Prayer.

JOURNEY OUTWARD

As you meet people today, try to be sensitive to the confusion in their lives. If you sense such chaos, pray for them but also be willing to lend a caring ear to listen to them. You may be God's creative agent to help bring order to their lives.

Be attentive also to world events or situations where confusion or chaos seems to be the ruling force. What would be needed to bring cosmos (God's harmony) to those situations?

JOURNEY IN GALILEE
HOPE OUT OF HOPELESSNESS

Preparation

Pray the whole *Te Deum* once again (see page 26). Let its rhythms begin to penetrate you and become part of you. This is a wonderful prayer to commit to memory because it forms us as we make it part of us.

Scripture: Read Mark 5:24b-34.

As you can see, Mark has again inserted one story into the middle of another. He begins the story of Jairus and his sick daughter, only to interrupt it with the story of the hemorrhaging woman. While taking this technique seriously, we will read each story separately.

JOURNEY INWARD
Hearing and Seeing

Reflect on the impossibility of each of the human situations Mark has shown us so far: the imminent drowning of the disciples in the storm, the hopeless insanity and possession of the man with the Legion, and now this woman who has "suffered much under many physicians, and had spent all that she had, and was no better but rather grew worse." What situations have you faced, or are you now facing, which seem hopeless to you?

Now reflect on how Jesus transforms hopelessness and chaos into hope and harmony in each case. Are you beginning to see Mark's point? How can you claim this authority of Jesus for your own hopeless difficulties?

Is the woman's faith, which Jesus commends, seen in her touching of his garment or in her confession in verse 33? Does it take more faith to hope for a magical cure or to tell Jesus "the whole truth"? Are you telling Christ the whole truth about your hopeless situation? You may want to write the truth of your hopeless situation here or in your journal.

Meditation and Prayer

Spend time in meditation, using any of the centering formulas or prayers which you have found helpful. Some teachers of meditation suggest looking at a picture or an object (a cross or crucifix is always appropriate) until you begin "looking through" the object, not focusing your attention on it but using it to help you focus your gaze inward to God. Another method is to close your eyes and focus on an imaginary black spot somewhere behind your eyes in the middle of your head. These are all merely techniques, of no value or importance in themselves, but simply aids to tune in to your inner space where God is waiting to meet you.

Think of one or two friends or family members whose situations are hopeless from a human point of view. Imagine them encountering Jesus. In your imagination, picture what he might say or do to them.

Conclude your time with the Lord's Prayer.

JOURNEY OUTWARD

Take your place today in the community of faith at worship. Every Sunday is a feast day, a "little Easter," and calls for rejoicing and celebrating rather than for penitence. Do something festive with your family or friends today, and "do all to the glory of God" (1 Cor. 10:31).

JOURNEY IN GALILEE
GRIEF INTO JOY

Preparation

Pray the prayer "St. Patrick's Breastplate." According to tradition this ancient prayer, its use in the church dating from about the ninth century, was originally inscribed on the breastplate of St. Patrick. It has become a treasured part of the church's heritage of prayer.

The Prayer of "St. Patrick's Breastplate"

I bind unto myself today
The strong name of the Trinity,
By invocation of the same,
The Three in One, and One in Three.

I bind this day to me forever,
By power of faith, Christ's Incarnation;
His baptism in the Jordan river;
His death on the cross for my salvation.
His bursting from the spicéd tomb;
His riding up the heav'nly way;
His coming at the day of doom:
I bind unto myself today.

I bind unto myself the power
Of the great love of cherubim;
The sweet "Well done" in judgment hour;
The service of the seraphim:
Confessors' faith, apostles' word,
The patriarchs' prayers, the prophets' scrolls;
All good deeds done unto the Lord,
And purity of virgin souls.

I bind unto myself today
The virtues of the starlit heav'n,
The glorious sun's life-giving ray,
The whiteness of the moon at even,
The flashing of the lightning free,
The whirling wind's tempestuous shocks,
The stable earth, the deep salt sea,
Around the old eternal rocks.

I bind unto myself today
The power of God to hold and lead,
His eye to watch, his might to stay,
His ear to hearken to my need;
The wisdom of my God to teach,
His hand to guide, his shield to ward;
The word of God to give me speech,
His heav'nly host to be my guard.

Christ be with me, Christ within me,
Christ behind me, Christ before me,
Christ beside me, Christ to win me,
Christ to comfort and restore me,
Christ beneath me, Christ above me,
Christ in quiet, Christ in danger,
Christ in hearts of all that love me,
Christ in mouth of friend and stranger.

I bind unto myself the Name,
The strong Name of the Trinity;
By invocation of the same,
The Three in One, and One in Three.
Of whom all nature hath creation;
Eternal Father, Spirit, Word:
Praise to the Lord of my salvation,
Salvation is of Christ the Lord.
Amen.

Scripture: Read Mark 5:21-24a, 35-43.

Notice that in Mark's order of telling the stories, there is a progression from a hopeless situation involving the impersonal and inanimate forces of nature (storm) to the more personal but supernatural forces of evil which affect a person (Gerasene demoniac) to the deeply personal matter of physical illness (hemorrhaging woman) to the most personal and most hopeless situation of all—death (Jairus's daughter).[9]

JOURNEY INWARD
Hearing and Seeing

Picture yourself among the crowd of mourners gathered at Jairus's house. If you had been there, what would your reaction have been to Jesus' announcement, "The child is not dead but sleeping"? Would you have joined in the scornful laughter? Why or why not?

Verse 42 says, "They were immediately overcome with amazement." Literally, the word translated *amazement* means "awe" or "dread." It is the kind of awe one experiences when confronted by an inexplicable power greater than one has ever encountered before. It is the fear of the holy. Have you ever experienced such a feeling? When? What meaning has it had for you?

Perhaps this story will speak to your fear of death. Such a fear is natural to human beings. Think of all the euphemisms we use to avoid using the word *dead* or *died* (for example, "passed away," "expired"). What might the Lord have to say to you in this story regarding your fear of death?

You might also want to think of death in this story as a metaphor for other terminal situations in life, such as the death of a friendship, a marriage, a dream. How might Jesus' authority over death manifest itself in your life? Reflect on these things in the space below.

Meditation and Prayer

Meditate for ten to fifteen minutes. Remember that Christian meditation differs from other forms in that its focus is not merely on self-control or self-transcendence but on an encounter with the living God at the deepest levels of the self. So let your meditation be the means by which you go inward to find God and experience God's love.

Imagine the "deaths" you have experienced in your life being transformed into resurrections by the power of the Risen Lord. Let these imaginings become prayer. Extend such prayers to friends and family members. Extend them further to include the situations in our world which are under the power of death and which need to be transfigured.

Conclude with the Lord's Prayer.

JOURNEY OUTWARD

Think of someone you know who has experienced a death—either the actual death of a loved one or the death of a relationship. Call or drop a note to that person, assuring him or her of your concern and love and also of the power of Christ to transform grief into joy.

JOURNEY IN GALILEE
HEALING THE HURTS OF REJECTION

Preparation

Start out today by praying the verse of "St. Patrick's Breastplate" which begins, "I bind this day to me forever, By power of faith, Christ's Incarnation" (see page 42). Reflect on how this verse covers the events of Jesus' life which have saving significance—his birth, baptism, death, resurrection, ascension, and coming again. Notice how the rhythm of our church year is built around these events. Because of its rhyme and rhythm, this prayer may be fairly easily memorized despite its length. You may only want to memorize parts of it.

Scripture: Read Mark 6:1-6.

This story carries forward Mark's theme of the misunderstanding and rejection of Jesus by those close to him. The motif of insiders/outsiders is at work here. By telling such stories, Mark forces the reader of his Gospel to question who the real insiders are.

JOURNEY INWARD
Hearing and Seeing

Anyone who has ever experienced rejection by close family and friends should find it easy to identify with Jesus as he was rejected in his hometown. Why did the people of his hometown synagogue "take offense" at him? What was the result of the rejection Jesus suffered by those close to him (verse 5)?

What experiences of rejection by people close to you have you had? Was your behavior responsible for the rejection or was the mindset of your friends or family responsible? How did you deal with the hurt you felt? Could you have prevented being rejected by conforming to the expectations of others? Would such compromise have made you feel better or worse? Reflect on these questions. Be as deeply honest with yourself as possible.

Meditation and Prayer

Let your reflections on personal experiences of rejection lead you to bring your hurt feelings to the Lord for healing. Are you willing to give up the feelings of resentment and anger you feel toward those who rejected you? Can you pray for the Lord's healing for them as well as for yourself? Are you willing to forgive the person(s) who rejected you?

When you have prayed sufficiently about this matter, move into a period of silence and meditational prayer. Bring yourself into God's presence and experience God's healing and forgiving and renewing love.

Conclude with the Lord's Prayer.

JOURNEY OUTWARD

Healing for the wounds we suffer when others reject us begins when we are willing to let go of the hurt and forgive the other. If we have been the rejecting one, we also are wounded and need to be forgiven in order to be healed. Seek out the person or persons who have rejected you or whom you have rejected and express your willingness to put the past behind you and make a new start in building a relationship.

JOURNEY IN GALILEE
RHYTHMS OF THE CHRISTIAN LIFE

Preparation

Use the verse ("I bind unto myself today The power . . .") of "St. Patrick's Breastplate" (see page 43). Notice how it concentrates on and affirms the reality of the community of saints. The writer of the Epistle to the Hebrews spoke of being "surrounded by so great a cloud of witnesses" (12:1). The preface to the Sanctus begins "And so, with your people on earth and all the company of heaven we praise your name and join their unending hymn." Remember as you begin to pray that you do not pray alone. Even when you are in solitude, you are praying in company.

Scripture: Read Mark 6:7-13, 30-32.

Notice in verses 12-13 how the mission of the disciples corresponds to the mission of Jesus and to the summary of that ministry in 1:15. Notice also how upon their return to Jesus they withdraw together to a lonely place, to the wilderness.

JOURNEY INWARD
Hearing and Seeing

Mark seems to be saying that the mission of Jesus' disciples is to be an extension of Jesus' own mission. Begin to reflect on your understanding of your own mission. In what conscious and deliberate ways have you attempted to be an extension of Jesus' mission in your own situation—at home, at work, in your neighborhood, at church?

What significance is there to the fact that a period of action (the disciples' mission) is followed by a period of retreat? How are you incorporating this rhythm of action/reflection or engagement/retreat in your own Christian life?

Meditation and Prayer

Meditate for ten minutes if possible. Use the Jesus Prayer (see page 23) or Abba Isaac's prayer formula (see page 17) to help you "descend with the mind into the heart." Breathe deeply and regularly as you use the mantra or meditation phrase. Do not think or form mental images; simply reach out in love to God with your spirit.

Now allow your mind to wander creatively and let these wanderings become the subject matter of your prayer. People, situations, and questions will stream through your consciousness. As they do, ask the Lord to help you see your mission to and with them.

Conclude with the Lord's Prayer.

JOURNEY OUTWARD

Try to be conscious of where the Lord might be sending you in mission. If you deliberately think of yourself as being sent by Christ, you will begin to discover where and to whom you are sent. Look at all your encounters today as opportunities for becoming an extension of Christ.

JOURNEY IN GALILEE
HEROD'S BANQUET OF DEATH

Preparation

Pray the verse of "St. Patrick's Breastplate" that begins "I bind unto myself . . . The virtues" (see page 42). This verse should help you "read" God's revelation in the creation around you. Remember that *lectio divina* includes this kind of reading. Praise God for the beauty of creation.

Scripture: Read Mark 6:14-29.

Using the technique of inserting one story into the middle of another, Mark interrupts the narrative about the disciples' mission to tell the story of a banquet thrown by King Herod. He weaves the two stories together by making the publicity surrounding the disciples' mission the occasion for Herod's taking an interest in Jesus and his followers. The story itself may have satisfied a natural curiosity in Mark's community as to the fate of John the Baptist. Mark's own interest in telling this story, however, will become clear when he tells the story of Jesus feeding the multitude. By juxtaposing these two stories, Mark contrasts the banquet of Herod which produces death and the banquet of Jesus which gives life and abundance.

JOURNEY INWARD
Hearing and Seeing

Despite King Herod's murder of John the Baptist, Mark does not present him as a totally evil person. Verse 20 tells us that Herod is in awe of John and has kept him safe, even if he did try to silence his denunciations of Herod's sin. Also, Herod regrets his rash promise to the daughter of Herodias, which results in John's death. In the story, Herod appears not so much wicked as weak. In the space below, reflect on those times in your life when weakness rather than malicious intent has caused you to do wrong or become involved in someone else's wrongdoing. What could you have done to produce a different result?

Meditation and Prayer

"Descend with the mind into the heart" by use of your centering prayer techniques. When you are focused, ask the Lord to reveal to you your weaknesses which lead you into destructive relationships or behaviors. As you become aware of these, imagine that Christ's strength is being given to you in each instance to take the place of your weakness. Ask for patience and the ability to forgive the weaknesses in others whom you love.

Conclude with the Lord's Prayer.

JOURNEY OUTWARD

Look around you today at some of the real evils you see in your community or even in your family. How many of them are due to weakness rather than wickedness? What action seems to be indicated to address one or more of these problems? If it is within your power, take whatever action is appropriate.

JOURNEY IN GALILEE
JESUS' FEAST OF LIFE

Preparation

Pray the verse of "St. Patrick's Breastplate" which begins "I bind . . . The power of God. . . ." (see page 43). This verse focuses on God's providence. Let this remind you that we are constantly in God's keeping and awareness. "If I take the wings of the morning and dwell in the uttermost parts of the sea, even there thy hand shall lead me, and thy right hand shall hold me" (Psalm 139:9).

Scripture: Read Mark 6:33-44.

What a contrast between the banquet Jesus provides for those who come to hear him and the banquet Herod provided for those who came to flatter him! Here Mark uses irony to contrast the disciples' success in their mission with their failure to provide food for the multitude, as well as to contrast the two banquets.

JOURNEY INWARD
Hearing and Seeing

Have you ever thought of the Christian life as a banquet? This image occurs not only in the story of Jesus' miraculous feeding of the multitude but also in John's story of the changing of the water into wine at the wedding feast in Cana (John 2:1-11). Spend a few moments reflecting on the abundance and richness of God's grace. At what points in your own journey of faith have you felt that Christ was feeding you a banquet?

Imagine yourself as a person with the opportunity/responsibility of feeding a hungry world with only five loaves and two fish. You can apply this reflection both to the world where physical hunger is real and to the world as it hungers for God, for truth, for justice, for peace. How can your small morsels contribute to the provision of enough and more than enough? Try to think as specifically as you can.

Meditation and Prayer

Meditate, using the prayer formulas or other techniques to help you move quickly to the place of inner stillness and awareness of God.

Gradually shift to mental or verbal prayers for others. Pray also that God will enable you to recognize your own gifts—your own morsels of food—which you may place at God's disposal.

Conclude with the Lord's Prayer.

JOURNEY OUTWARD

If you have chosen to fast on Fridays, this will be a fasting day for you.

Take one of your own "loaves and fishes" and share it with someone. It could be a note expressing caring and concern for a friend or relative who is going through a difficult time. It could be a word of apology and confession to someone you've wronged or the offer of forgiveness and reconciliation to someone who has wronged you. It could be a donation to UMCOR (United Methodist Committee on Relief) or some other organization which combats hunger. The point is to do something that is going to help Christ provide his banquet.

JOURNEY IN GALILEE
IN THE SAME BOAT WITH THE DISCIPLES

Preparation

Pray the verse of "St. Patrick's Breastplate" which begins, "Christ be with me
. . ." (see page 43). This is an invocation to Christ, asking him to envelop us completely. This prayer will help us realize more fully the meaning of St. Paul's phrase,
"Christ in you, the hope of glory" (Col. 1:27). The introduction of "friend and
stranger" in the last line prevents this from being conceived purely as an individual
and private matter. When enveloped by Christ, we are in community with both the
friend and the stranger.

Scripture: Read Mark 6:45-52.

Notice in verse 46 Jesus' withdrawal from his public ministry for prayer. There is
the wilderness motif again. The story of Jesus appearing on the sea while his
disciples were in the boat may be a variant of the story of the storm at sea in chapter
4, or it may be based on another incident. By itself, the story has no links with the
feeding story, but in Mark's hands it becomes a commentary on the failure of the
disciples to feed the multitudes.

JOURNEY INWARD
Hearing and Seeing

Reflect on the reaction of the disciples to Jesus walking on the water (verses
49-51). Why might they have responded with such fear? Mark seems to link their
fear with their failure to feed the multitude at Jesus' command. What does this say to
you about the relationship of fear and unbelief?

At what points in your life has your fear or anxiety resulted from your failure to do what you knew God wanted you to do? To what extent was your failure itself the result of fear? What is the thing you fear most right now?

Is your fear blocking your faith? Imagine that you are in the same boat with the disciples (which is exactly Mark's point: we are all "in the same boat") and you hear Jesus' words to you, "Take heart, it is I; have no fear." Confess your fears in your journal, or write them in the space provided. You may even find it helpful to confess your greatest fear to someone you trust. Owning up to our fears is the first step toward liberation from them.

Meditation and Prayer

In your meditation today, let Jesus' words to his fearful disciples become his words to you. Repeat that sentence, "Take heart, it is I; have no fear," slowly again and again. Say the first phrase, "Take heart, it is I," as you inhale and "have no fear" as you exhale. Let this prayer begin to drive out your fear.

Pray for someone you know who is bound by fear, whose fear is causing him or her to fail in important ways. Pray for others whose needs you know.

Conclude with the Lord's Prayer.

JOURNEY OUTWARD

If you have the opportunity, confront the situation that terrifies you most and take some deliberate action to overcome that fear. As you do this, depend on Christ's presence in the boat with you.

JOURNEY IN GALILEE
INNER DEFILEMENTS

Preparation

Pray the whole prayer of "St. Patrick's Breastplate," being particularly aware of the first and the last invocations of the Trinity (see pages 42 and 43). Reflect on how the various parts of the prayer emphasize the work of the three Persons of the Holy Trinity. Give thanks for the richness of God's self-revelation.

Scripture: Read Mark 7:1-23.

The practice of *corban* (verse 11), against which Jesus speaks so harshly, was conceived as a legal loophole in the religious law. The law commanded that a son should be financially responsible for his parents in their old age. Another command forbade the personal use of anything which had been dedicated to God. So the practice evolved whereby a person who wished to evade his responsibility to his aged parents could take the portion of his money which would normally have gone to them and "dedicate" (*corban*) it to God, thereby making it impossible to be used by his parents. While technically adhering to the law, this practice was the product of greed and self-interest, inner qualities which defile a person.

JOURNEY INWARD
Hearing and Seeing

Think about the rationalizations we sometimes use to avoid doing what we know we ought to do. From what inner defilement do such rationalizations spring?

What is it that "comes out" of you that is spiritually defiling? When you can identify these inner qualities and attitudes, you will have put your finger on the places where you need to be converted. We can never get from Galilee to Caesarea Philippi (the place of conversion) until we have identified the areas where conversion is needed.

Meditation and Prayer

Confess to God in prayer, and perhaps to your journal as well, your inner defilements. Picture yourself standing with Jesus and telling him about them. Do they become more or less evil when you do this? Now picture what Jesus is saying to you as you tell him about each of the things that "comes out of you." Accept his love and forgiveness.

Meditate in inner silence. If you are finding that this silence is becoming more important to you, you may want to lengthen the time you spend in meditation. Adjust the time to fit your capacity and need. Remain alert to God, however. Don't let your silence become slackness. If you feel yourself sinking into inattention or sleepiness, use words of prayer to renew your inner stillness and alertness to God.

Pray for those whom your own inner defilements may have hurt or injured.

Pray for the peace of the world, our national and international leaders, our enemies, and our friends.

Conclude with the Lord's Prayer.

JOURNEY OUTWARD

In all your encounters today, try to be sensitive to the inner qualities and attitudes which are revealed by words and outward actions, both in yourself and other people.

Go to church to worship today. Remember that you are part of the Body of Christ, and so you must take seriously your responsibility to the whole Body. As you worship, try to maintain an attitude of prayerful expectation that the Holy Spirit will have freedom to guide and direct the community of believers. If you are doing today's part of the Lenten journey in the evening, then pray for the guidance and direction of the Holy Spirit in your own congregation or parish and in your denomination, and then pray for the church universal in all its forms throughout this country and the world.

JOURNEY IN GALILEE
THE CRUMBS FROM THE TABLE

Preparation

Come to your time of prayer expectantly. Use this prayer often attributed to St. Francis of Assisi as both an invocation of God's presence and a consecration of yourself.

> Lord, make me an instrument of your peace.
> Where there is hatred, let me sow love,
> Where there is injury, pardon,
> Where there is doubt, faith,
> Where there is despair, hope,
> Where there is darkness, light,
> And where there is sadness, joy.
>
> O Divine Master, grant that I may not so much seek
>   to be consoled as to console,
> not so much to be understood as to understand,
> not so much to be loved, as to love;
> for it is in giving that we receive,
> it is in pardoning that we are pardoned,
> it is in dying, that we are born to eternal life.

Scripture: Read Mark 7:24-30.

Mark uses this story for contrast with the previous one. Whereas the religious leaders of Israel have made a mockery of the religious law and thereby proved they are spiritually defiled, this Gentile woman, whom the Israelites would have considered as defiled, is really the one who is spiritually pure. While the religious leaders find fault with Jesus, she desires only what he can do for her.

JOURNEY INWARD
Hearing and Seeing

What people or group of people have you either consciously or unconsciously considered as "dogs"? In other words, to whom do you consider yourself superior? On what basis does your supposed superiority rest—race, ethnic identity, economic class, educational differences, political party, gender, or religion? You must be ruthlessly honest at this point.

Perhaps you identify more with the Syrophoenician woman in the story. You have experienced feeling rejected and treated as an outcast by others, either because of your behavior, your looks, your ethnic background, your financial position, or some other reason. Reflect on how the woman in the story deals with the fact that she is despised by others. Does she let such rejection prevent her from experiencing Christ's healing grace? Do you?

Meditation and Prayer

Confess to God the times you feel superiority and contempt for others and the times you feel rejected by others. Allow the "crumbs" from Christ's table to fall on your plate. Remember that Christ offers us not "crumbs" but a banquet!

Pray for your own and others' needs as your thoughts are led to them.

Conclude with the Lord's Prayer.

JOURNEY OUTWARD

In your newspaper or a newsmagazine, try to find an article that deals with the problems faced by people who belong to a group you've always classified as "dogs"—poor inner city people, rich Wall Street bankers, a new group of immigrants, or others. Try, as much as you are able, to imagine those problems from their perspective. As often as you can throughout the day, lift up a prayer for the people about whom you've read. Begin to ask yourself: Is there anything I can be or do to address the problems faced by others whose existence I am now acknowledging?

JOURNEY IN GALILEE
SPIRITUAL DEAFNESS

Preparation

Find your quiet place and time and settle yourself in expectation of meeting God. Use the Prayer of St. Francis of Assisi again to help recollect yourself (see page 59). Think of all the qualities you are asking God to manifest through your life—peace, love, pardon, faith, hope, light, joy, consolation, understanding. Can you pray for these things honestly?

Scripture: Read Mark 7:31-37.

This story and the one in 8:22-26 are especially significant. In 4:10-12, Mark used the quotation from Isaiah to speak of those who "see and see but do not see, who hear and hear but do not hear" (AT). Mark's special use of the imagery of hearing and seeing as ways in which God's revelation in Jesus is apprehended is prominent in both stories. In this story, a deaf man, who ostensibly cannot "hear" Jesus, is healed of his deafness. This healing, which involves more than a physical defect, results in zealous proclamation. The story of the disciples in 8:14-21 will serve as a contrast both to this story and to the one in 8:22-26.

JOURNEY INWARD
Hearing and Seeing

Think about the things in your life which prevent you from "hearing" the word of Christ. What are the causes of your spiritual deafness? Some written reflection in your journal over a period of days may be helpful at this point.

What is the connection between hearing and speaking in your life? Does God's word, when heard, have an effect upon what we communicate to others?

Meditation and Prayer

Meditate in silence for fifteen or twenty minutes. In your silent alertness before God, seek to hear what God is saying to you. Drowning out the noise of the distractions and illusions of your false self will be necessary to hear the "still, small voice" which comes into your silence.

Pray for the needs of others as they enter your consciousness. You might want to imagine the other person coming to Christ with his or her needs, and then "see" the light and radiance of Christ enveloping him or her, bringing wholeness and joy.

Conclude with the Lord's Prayer.

JOURNEY OUTWARD

Listen, really listen, to what members of your family or your neighbors are saying to you today, both in their spoken words and in their actions. Listen for the deeper, unspoken meanings behind what they say. Listen for their calls for help, their desire to love and be loved, and their aspirations and confessions of failure. Be there for them!

JOURNEY IN GALILEE
THE COMPASSION OF CHRIST

Preparation

Reflect for a moment on the phrase *Lord, make me an instrument of your peace.* The opposite of peace is confusion, disorder, chaos. Remember that you are here in the Lord's presence to have your own inner conflicts healed, for only as your own wounds are being healed can you become an instrument of the Lord's healing for others.

Scripture: Read Mark 8:1-10.

Most scholars agree that this story is a variant of the earlier feeding story in chapter 6. It may have circulated orally in the traditions about Jesus before Mark used it in his Gospel. However, Mark himself is certainly responsible for including it. He undoubtedly recognized it as a variant of the earlier story, but it suited his purpose to tell it again because it emphasizes the continuing spiritual blindness of the disciples. You will have noticed that Mark treats the disciples rather negatively, much more so than do Matthew or Luke. Mark may present this picture of the disciples as a way of making the point to members of his own community that they should not be discouraged when they find it difficult to have faith, since even the disciples found this difficult.

JOURNEY INWARD
Hearing and Seeing

Reflect on the different responses of Jesus and his disciples to the hunger of the crowd. Jesus has compassion; his disciples are realists. They recognize the impossibility of feeding such a large number of people with such meager resources. How do you respond to needs of other people when you become aware of them? Do you see the situation as one which has great possibilities for the exercise of faith? Or are you a realist, saying, "It's a shame the way things are, but what can one person do?" Write about a time when you responded in one of these ways.

Seven loaves in the hands of pragmatic and—yes, let's say it—faithless disciples are certainly not enough to feed a multitude. In the hands of Jesus, blessed with compassion and faith in God's power, they become a feast which not only is sufficient but also produces seven baskets of leftovers. What is the equivalent of the seven loaves in your life?

As you reflect on what those seven loaves are in your life, consciously turn them over to Christ. Ask him to take those gifts, abilities, interests, resources, or whatever they may be and use them to feed a multitude.

Meditation and Prayer

Spend time in meditation, reaching out to embrace the Lord in love. Mentally imagine Christ making himself at home in your life, opening all the hidden doors and filling every corner with his love and grace. Don't forget to let him sweep up the cobwebs in the corners.

Ask God to give you the compassion of Christ. Such compassion is not a sentimental feeling; it is a habit of life which leads to attitude and action.

Pray for those needs of others that you are aware of. Remember that you do not pray alone; you are in the company of all the saints.

Conclude with the Lord's Prayer.

JOURNEY OUTWARD

As you go about your work today, keep your eyes open for situations in which your compassionate action could make a difference. Your compassionate act may be a personal act directed toward one other person who is struggling, or it might involve joining in some corporate expressions of Christian compassion such as volunteering for a church ministry to the hungry or homeless. But look! Whatever you do, begin to form the habit of *compassionate seeing*.

JOURNEY IN GALILEE
THICKHEADED DISCIPLES

Preparation

Reflect briefly on the pairs of opposites in the Prayer of St. Francis: hatred/love; injury/pardon; doubt/faith; despair/hope; sadness/joy. Pray the prayer with special awareness of the movements in your own life from one pole to the other of these paired opposites.

Scripture: Read Mark 8:11-12.

Mark's literary skill may be seen clearly in this passage. By mentioning the disciples' obsession with their lack of bread, he links the story with the story of Jesus' feeding miracle in its two tellings and paints an unflattering portrait of the disciples at the same time. Jesus' question to the disciples in verse 18 recalls the saying about the purpose of the parables in Mark 4:10-12. And the mention of both "seeing" and "hearing" connects this story with the stories of the healing of the deaf man in chapter 7 and the healing of the blind man in chapter 8.

JOURNEY INWARD
Hearing and Seeing

Have you ever been frustrated by the response of your spouse, your children, or a friend when you have gone to some pains to make something clear and yet they have failed to grasp your point? Now picture yourself "in the same boat" with the disciples. How could they be so thickheaded as to miss Jesus' point? How can we?

How keen are your spiritual hearing and eyesight? In what areas of your life are you becoming aware of blind spots or deafness to God's voice?

Meditation and Prayer

Continue your practice in meditative prayer, focusing your inner self on love for God. After a time of attentive silence, try reflecting in your journal on some of the blind spots in your own life. As you become aware of these, ask the Lord to heal your deaf ears and your blind eyes.

Pray for others as you are led.
Conclude with the Lord's Prayer.

JOURNEY OUTWARD

Listen to someone you've never really listened to before. That someone may be your husband or wife, one of your children, an in-law, an elderly aunt, or a cranky neighbor. Tune in the ears of your mind and heart to hear what others are saying to you, perhaps without words. As you hear them "speak" to you, lift them up in prayer.

JOURNEY IN GALILEE
PARTIAL SIGHT

Preparation

In addition to using the Prayer of St. Francis (see page 59), you may also find helpful singing a favorite hymn or listening to a piece of music that will draw you into an attitude of prayer and inner stillness before God.

Scripture: Read Mark 8:22-26.

This is one of the most important passages in the Gospel. It serves as a transition from the journey of Jesus in Galilee to his journey to Jerusalem, and it leads directly to the turning point of the Gospel in 8:27-30. In all likelihood, the two-stage healing of the blind man is Mark's own creation. The story of the healing of a blind man came to him from his sources, but the idea of the restoration first of partial sight and then of full sight may be Mark's own interpretation of the event. If so, it will provide a significant clue to what Mark is saying not only about how the disciples (we may include ourselves, too) encounter Jesus but also about how to read this Gospel. Might it be read on more than one level? Keep this possibility in mind as we go on.

JOURNEY INWARD
Hearing and Seeing

Think of a specific time in your spiritual journey when you were like the man after the first touch by Jesus—you had partial sight, but you really didn't see "everything clearly." Perhaps you are still at that stage. Can you remember a point at which you felt that Christ had given you a second touch? Was there a sudden insight into yourself, a new understanding of how God is working in your life, a liberation from an enslaving habit, or a breaking out of old patterns of behavior? In what areas of your life do you now need a second touch?

John Wesley, the father of Methodism, received such a second touch, and it set him free to become the spiritual dynamo who transformed England in the eighteenth century. For years, Wesley had been a pious and devoted Christian, a priest in the Church of England. He had pursued a holy life with such purpose and method that he and his friends were given the derogatory name "Methodists." Yet, at one essential point, he remained blind: he did not feel the assurance in his spirit that God had accepted him and claimed him. Here is his description of his second touch:

> And accordingly, the next day he [Peter Böhler, a Moravian friend of Wesley who was instrumental in his second touch] came again with three others, all of whom testified, of their own personal experience, that a true living faith in Christ is inseparable from a sense of pardon for all past and freedom from all present sins. They added with one mouth that this faith was the gift, the free gift of God; and that He would surely bestow it upon every soul who earnestly and perseveringly sought it. I was now thoroughly convinced; and, by the grace of God, I resolved to seek it unto the end, (1) By absolutely renouncing all dependence, in whole or in part, upon *my own* works or righteousness; . . . (2) by adding to the constant use of all the other means of grace, continual prayer for this very thing, justifying, saving faith, a full reliance on the blood of Christ shed for me; a trust in Him, as *my* Christ, as *my* sole justification, sanctification, and redemption. . . . In the evening [of May 24, 1738] I went very unwillingly to a society in Aldersgate Street, where one was reading Luther's preface to the *Epistle to the Romans*. About a quarter before nine, while he was describing the change which God works in the heart through faith in Christ, I felt my heart strangely warmed. I felt I did trust in Christ, Christ alone for my salvation; and an assurance was given me that He had taken away *my* sins, even *mine*, and saved *me* from the law of sin and death.[10]

Meditation and Prayer

Enter into your period of meditation. This time, picture yourself encountering Jesus in the silence. He knows that your sight is dim, partial, veiled. Picture Christ coming to you and laying his hands on your eyes a second time. Open yourself as fully as possible to this healing touch.

As you pray for others today, pray also for some situation or person or group of people in the larger world where human blindness is causing strife or suffering.

Conclude with the Lord's Prayer.

68

JOURNEY OUTWARD

Pray this prayer throughout the day: "Where there is darkness, let me bring light." Try to become aware today of situations where blindness through ignorance or willful refusal to see is keeping someone in darkness. Pray to know what you can do to bring the Lord's light into that situation. If it is a situation in your home or family or at work, perhaps some loving confrontation will be necessary. If it is a more public issue of social justice, perhaps you will need to write your representatives in Congress or some other public official to make your views known.

If you have chosen to fast on Fridays, keep in mind the appropriate ways and cautions mentioned earlier (see page 21).

DAY 25

JOURNEY AT CAESAREA PHILIPPI
THE CALL TO DECISION

Preparation

Again use the Prayer of St. Francis of Assisi (see page 59) to recollect yourself and put yourself at God's disposal. Give a few moments to the petition "Where there is injury, [let me sow] pardon." What injuries have you suffered for which you need to forgive someone? In God's presence, let them go and be free.

Scripture: Read Mark 8:27-30.

This passage marks the turning point in Mark's Gospel. From this point on, Jesus' disciples are more in focus than the crowds. Jesus begins to direct his attention and teaching to those who were his closest followers. For Mark, Caesarea Philippi is not only a place on the map. It is a point on a pilgrimage as well. It is the place of decision, commitment, insight, and revelation. It is at Caesarea Philippi that Jesus asks his disciples the crucial question, "Who do you say that I am?"

JOURNEY INWARD
Hearing and Seeing

In telling the story of Jesus calling his disciples to a point of decision, Mark is also calling his readers, both the original readers and all subsequent readers of the Gospel, to the same point of decision. In effect, Mark is saying, "All right, now you've seen and heard this man Jesus as he has gone about Galilee teaching and preaching. You've witnessed the authority of his words and his life. Now it's decision time. Who is he for you?"

Put yourself into the story. Let Jesus address you: "Who do *you* say that I am?" Don't treat this as a theological question. Rather, let it be a personal question addressed to you at the point in your own journey to which you have come. Who is Jesus for you right now? Is he a figment of your imagination? A threat? Someone whom you would rather ignore? Is he a rather vague but comforting presence? Is he your Lord?

Peter's confession, "You are the Messiah" (AT), was sincere, even if not clearly understood. Perhaps, like Peter, you are only beginning to "see" who Jesus is for you. Do you have the faith of Peter to make the confession, even if you're not totally certain?

Meditation and Prayer

In silence, picture yourself taking Christ on a tour of your life. As you enter each room (work, family, church, social gatherings, personal habits, etc.), let him ask you the decisive question, "Who do you say that I am in this room?" Are there any rooms you don't want Christ to enter? Why not?

Now bring to mind those whom you love most. Who do you want Christ to be for them? Reflect on ways in which you might be influencing their answer to the question. As you summon up each person in your mind's eye, see yourself bringing him or her to Jesus for whatever encounter of faith he or she needs.

Conclude with the Lord's Prayer.

JOURNEY OUTWARD

Seek out the person you most want to see touched by Christ. In some concrete way, by word or action, let her or him know of your love, your forgiveness (if reconciliation is needed), and your commitment to that person. You may find enriching the sharing of your own journey with her or him and relating what you are learning about who Jesus is for you.

THE LORD'S DAY

JOURNEY AT CAESAREA PHILIPPI
THE CONFRONTATION WITH ILLUSION

Preparation

Once again, pray the Prayer of St. Francis of Assisi (see page 59). You may also find helpful singing a favorite hymn or listening to a piece of music that will draw you into an attitude of prayer and inner stillness before God. The hymnal is a wonderful aid to prayer.

Scripture: Read Mark 8:31-33.

This passage is the first of the so-called "Passion predictions" in Mark's Gospel. The short formula, where the entire Passion narrative is summed up, is used effectively three times at crucial points in the narrative to highlight both the true meaning of Jesus and the disciples' blindness to that meaning. In each instance, the prediction calls the disciples away from illusion to the sober reality of redemptive suffering.

JOURNEY INWARD
Hearing and Seeing

Why, when Jesus announces "plainly" that he is going up to Jerusalem and will meet with rejection and death there, does Peter react negatively? Why does his reaction provoke an even stronger rebuke from Jesus?

What illusions do you cherish regarding your life? What unrealistic expectations or visions of your future have you embraced that are preventing you from following Jesus along the same road that he is walking? What will giving up these illusions mean for you?

Meditation and Prayer

After a time of centering silence, imagine what Jesus would say to you if he were to "speak plainly" about the path he wants you as his disciple to follow. You may want to record in your journal or in the space provided Jesus' words to you as well as your reply to him. When you feel able, bring those illusions you've identified in yourself, discard them in Christ's presence, and accept your reality in the freedom Christ gives you.

Conclude your time with the Lord's Prayer.

JOURNEY OUTWARD

Join the community of faith at prayer today. Remember that you are part of the Body of Christ, and take seriously your responsibility to the whole Body.

Deliberately seek out someone in church whom you don't know and introduce yourself to that person. Try to really listen to and begin to know him or her.

JOURNEY AT CAESAREA PHILIPPI
THE COST OF DISCIPLESHIP

Preparation

Withdraw to your place of prayer. Go joyfully, not grudgingly. Remind yourself that you are going to meet God. Sing softly the first verse of "Sweet Hour of Prayer."

> Sweet hour of prayer! sweet hour of prayer!
> That calls me from a world of care,
> And bids me at my Father's throne
> Make all my wants and wishes known.
> In seasons of distress and grief,
> My soul has often found relief,
> And oft escaped the tempter's snare
> By thy return, sweet hour of prayer!

Scripture: Read Mark 8:34–9:1.

In verses 9:31 and 10:33 we find the other two occurrences of the "passion predictions." In each of the repetitions of this formula concerning the sufferings of the Son of Man, the emphasis is on the fact that it is Jesus speaking to his disciples. Significant also is that in all three instances, Jesus' disciples fail to understand what he is saying to them, thus demonstrating that they do not yet see everything clearly.

JOURNEY INWARD
Hearing and Seeing

There is a threefold movement to the decision to be a disciple, and it is the same movement that Jesus himself had to experience in order to fulfill his own vocation. *Self-denial, cross-bearing,* and *following* constitute this movement of the spiritual life.

Self-denial does not mean self-hatred or self-disparagement. It means taking self (ego) off the throne of my life in order that I may lose my self-centeredness and thus find my true self in God (verse 35). What would this mean for you in specific terms? What are the areas of your life which you insist on controlling? Where are you still reigning as Lord?

Taking up the cross was a very specific act for Jesus. It can be no less specific for his followers. For Jesus, it meant accepting suffering and death, not stoically and in resignation, but consciously and freely as an act of consecration to doing the will of God. It was that act of freedom which transformed the cross into something redemptive rather than something ultimately destructive. What will it mean for you to take up the cross? What would a cruciform (cross-shaped) life look like for you? You may wish first to draw a cruciform and then to write your reflections inside the shape.

The word *follow* is Mark's special word for discipleship. A disciple is one who follows Jesus. In the context of Jesus' teaching about his sufferings and in light of the first two movements of self-denial and cross-bearing, the word *follow* gains a specific meaning. *To follow Jesus* means to take the same road, make the same kinds of choices, face the possibility of the same end he did. For his earliest disciples, that often meant following to their own deaths as martyrs. For us, who live in a much more tolerant society, it may not mean execution in a literal sense, but it must be given specific content.

Following is an action. What will it mean for you to follow Jesus? Where is your point of departure? What road will you travel as you walk in his footsteps? If you can see no cross on the road, you may be on the wrong road, following some other leader.

Meditation and Prayer

Caesarea Philippi is a crucial symbolic point in all our journeys. It is the point of decision and commitment. Whether we are ever healed of our blindness and deafness will depend on what road we take from Caesarea Philippi.

Reflect prayerfully on verses 34-35. Let Jesus' words call you to commitment. If you are ready to move on with Jesus from Caesarea Philippi, tell him so. Perhaps the words of the old spiritual will help you express your commitment:

> I have decided to follow Jesus
> I have decided to follow Jesus
> I have decided to follow Jesus
> No turning back, no turning back.
>
> The world behind me, the cross before me
> The world behind me, the cross before me
> The world behind me, the cross before me
> No turning back, no turning back.

The road of discipleship may lead to the cross, but on it we are always given "songs in the night." If you have committed yourself, make that commitment more concrete by recording it in your journal. Come back to it from time to time, especially when the road gets foggy or steep. Your written record will remind you of the stake you have driven at Caesarea Philippi.

Conclude with the Lord's Prayer.

JOURNEY OUTWARD

Plan to watch television for an hour or two today if possible. If today is not convenient, carry over this assignment until tomorrow. Write down (either below or in your journal) what values, life-styles, and calls to discipleship are being projected, both in the programs and in the commercials. Through these, what road are you being asked to travel? What lord are you being asked to follow? By identifying the alternatives, you will gain increasing understanding of what following Jesus will entail in the real world in which you live. Write down your reflections and conclusions about what values or life-styles you may need to leave behind in following Jesus.

THE TRANSFIGURATION

JOURNEY ON THE MOUNTAINTOP
GLIMPSES OF GLORY

Preparation

Pray this prayer of St. Thomas Aquinas. Reflect on the power and freedom that would be yours if your heart were like the heart St. Thomas prayed for.

Give me, O Lord, a steadfast heart, which no unworthy thought can drag downward; an unconquered heart, which no tribulation can wear out; an upright heart, which no unworthy purpose may tempt aside.

Bestow upon me also, O Lord my God, understanding to know thee, diligence to seek thee, wisdom to find thee, and a faithfulness that may finally embrace thee; through Jesus Christ our Lord. Amen.

Scripture: Read Mark 9:2-13.

Some scholars have felt that the Transfiguration story in Mark 9 was really a resurrection appearance, projected by Mark back into the period of the ministry of Jesus. This view arose because Mark reports no resurrection appearances. Various theories have been offered to explain such an omission on Mark's part, but little agreement has been reached. The meaning of the story in Mark's use of it is that Jesus' vocation as Messiah, confessed by Peter and the others at Caesarea Philippi, is here given divine affirmation. It is testified to by Moses and Elijah, representing the Law and the Prophets of the Old Covenant. Visual and auditory imagery is also prominent in the story: the disciples "see" Jesus glorified and "hear" a heavenly voice commanding them to "listen" to Jesus.

JOURNEY INWARD
Hearing and Seeing

In all of our journeys, there are times when, for a moment at least, we are given glimpses of glory. Sudden insights into ourselves or into God flood our consciousness. We have been plodding along, and suddenly we make a breakthrough to a new level of love, joy, faith, courage, or hope. Maybe a retreat or a conference we've attended has been such a high point for us. Perhaps some inner conflict has been resolved. Maybe on one particular day, our prayer ceased to be a discipline and we found ourselves caught up in rapture and overwhelmed by God's nearness. Maybe the euphoria of receiving some longed-for good news or the birth of a new grandchild has given us a real shot-in-the-arm spiritually. All of us have had such mountaintop experiences. Go back in your memory to one mountaintop experience in your own life. Relive the event and your reaction. Was it predictable, or did you experience it as a gift?

The disciples wanted to stay up there on the mountaintop with the transfigured Jesus. They wanted to build houses and live there. But Jesus led them down from the mountain just as he had led them up. What does this say to you about the nature of the spiritual life? Is it reasonable to expect that we should always be gazing on glory? We often make the mistake of the disciples, wishing we could stay "high" with Jesus. However, life goes on in the valley of human need, and that is where we must live. High points of religious experience are given to illuminate or transfigure the valleys where we live out our discipleship.

Meditation and Prayer

In your prayer, as you remember your mountaintops, give thanks for them as God's gifts to you to help you prepare for the hard road of discipleship. Let the memory of those moments of spiritual insight or revelation renew you for the journey in the valley of daily life.

Enter into a period of attentive silence so that you can do what the heavenly voice commanded: listen to Jesus. You may want to keep your journal or a piece of paper close by so that you can write down what you "hear."

Conclude with the Lord's Prayer.

JOURNEY OUTWARD

Today is a fasting day for you, if you have chosen to fast on Fridays. As part of your journey outward, begin to investigate what concrete things you can do to make an impact upon the problem of hunger in the world. Find out what church agencies for hunger relief you can support. Perhaps you will want to subscribe to "Bread," the newsletter of the organization Bread for the World to find out what this Christian legislative-action group is doing to promote legislation in Congress that will benefit hungry people. Write your representatives or senators, urging them to vote for food-aid bills that are before them. Spend some time praying for hungry people.

JOURNEY IN THE VALLEY
FAITH AND UNBELIEF

Preparation

Again, pray the prayer of St. Thomas Aquinas (see page 78). See this prayer as a weapon against self-deception or shallowness. Dwell on each of its petitions until they begin to become your own.

Scripture: Read Mark 9:14-29.

Mark returns in this story to his theme of the blindness of the disciples. By placing it immediately after the story of the mountaintop experience of the Transfiguration, Mark makes the failure of the disciples' faith even more striking. In a way, Mark's portrayal of the disciples gives us hope. Theirs is what William Stringfellow has called "exemplary disbelief." If Jesus' own disciples were so slow to grasp what it means to follow Jesus, there is hope for us also.

JOURNEY INWARD
Hearing and Seeing

Focus on Jesus' statement and the father's response, "All things are possible to him who believes" (verse 23). "I believe; help my unbelief!" (verse 24) Here are both the promise and the dilemma of discipleship. Reflect on the times or situations in your life when you have exhibited just such a mixture of faith and unfaith. Where is this tension most evident in your life?

Did this mixture of faith and unbelief on the part of the father either prevent or hinder Jesus from healing his son? Should it prevent Christ from casting out the unclean spirits from your life? The important thing is to be aware of the amount of belief there is within you even when you are most wanting to have faith.

Reflect on Jesus' reply to the disciples in verse 29. What is the link between spiritual authority and prayer? We didn't see Jesus making a specific prayer on this occasion, so prayer must mean more than some specific words said on a specific occasion. In other words, it is not saying prayers that is in focus here but a way of life, a whole orientation of our being. How are you beginning to sense that this experiment in re-orienting your life holds the key to spiritual integrity and power?

What particular valley are you going through now? Do you see where your unbelief is blocking the flow of God's energy and renewal? Can you pray the father's prayer: "Lord, I believe; help my unbelief"?

Meditation and Prayer

Spend time in meditation. Use one of the prayer formulas you have learned or one of your own choosing. Apply rhythmical breathing to aid you in achieving inner stillness before God.

Conclude your time with the Lord's Prayer.

JOURNEY OUTWARD

What valleys are there around you in the larger world? Where do you see the unclean spirits exerting their mastery over human beings? Read your newspaper or a newsmagazine with this perspective in mind. Where are faith and prayer called for on your part in any of this? What authoritative action is within your power to take? Pray for God's strength to act where you perceive the Lord wants you to take action.

JOURNEY IN THE VALLEY
MISUNDERSTANDING AND FEAR

Preparation

Once more pray the prayer of St. Thomas Aquinas (see page 78). Dwell on the petitions for understanding, diligence, wisdom, and faithfulness.

Scripture: Read Mark 9:30-32.

This passage is Mark's second use of Jesus' announcement of his coming Passion. Verse 32 reiterates the theme of the disciples' blindness.

JOURNEY INWARD
Hearing and Seeing

Why do you think the disciples were afraid to ask Jesus what he meant by the announcement that the Son of Man was going to be killed and then rise again? Could it have been a fear of appearing stupid? Could it have been a fear that they would be involved in his sufferings, sharing his fate?

When you think of Jesus' statement that discipleship involves the triple movement of *self-denial, cross-bearing,* and *following,* what feelings does it evoke in you? Is fear among them? If so, what is it that you're afraid of? Write these fears in the space below. Sometimes when we are able to identify our fears—to name them—we are more able to discover the power, through God's assistance, to overcome them.

Meditation and Prayer

After spending some time in silence and centering, let the fears which you have identified surface in God's healing presence. You may find it helpful to imagine yourself bringing your fear to the feet of Christ, laying it down, and walking away from it, thus giving it to him. Or you may envision Christ himself looking you directly in the eye and saying quietly, yet authoritatively, "Fear not." However it is most meaningful to you, try to let go of those fears and give them to the Lord.

JOURNEY OUTWARD

As you read your newspaper or watch the news on TV today, try to be sensitive to how many troubled situations are the result of fear—the fear of individuals or nations or public leaders. What does your faith have to say to these situations?

JOURNEY IN THE VALLEY
CHILDLIKE FAITH

Preparation

Use the following prayer of St. Ignatius of Loyola for your preparation. In today's scripture reading there is a saying of Jesus being "last of all" and "servant of all." This prayer of St. Ignatius will help you hear these sayings more clearly.

Teach us, good Lord, to serve thee as thou deservest; to give and not to count the cost; to fight and not to heed the wounds; to toil and not to seek for rest; to labor and not to ask for any reward, save that of knowing that we do thy will; through Jesus Christ our Lord. Amen.

Scripture: Read Mark 9:33-41.

Mark contrasts Jesus' commendation of child*like* faith with the disciples' child*ish* behavior in wanting to be the greatest and in wanting exclusive rights to Jesus' authority over evil spirits.

JOURNEY INWARD
Hearing and Seeing

Mark uses the saying "Whoever receives one such child in my name receives me" as an illustration of the paradox "If anyone would be first, he must be last of all and servant of all." What is the connection? Why is receiving a child equated with receiving Christ? Ponder this statement and ask yourself, Who or what are the "children" I must receive? How is Christ someone who must be received? What connection is there between receiving and following?

What does it mean to do something *in the name of Christ?* What does this phrase suggest about our motivation? About our authority?

Meditation and Prayer

Begin your prayer time today by singing a hymn softly. Choose one that is meditative and quiet and which speaks to you. Follow this by a time of letting your spirit flow out to God in love and praise. Confess your child*ish* attitudes and behavior patterns and begin to pray for true child*like* faith to receive and follow Christ.

Conclude with the Lord's Prayer.

JOURNEY OUTWARD

As you go through the day, take a break now and then to ask yourself which of your activities you could honestly say you've done "in the name of Christ." Consciously try to approach each situation with that motivation and authority. Keep track in your journal of your experiment.

If you have chosen to fast each Friday during Lent, make your mealtimes times of self-assessment and journaling.

JOURNEY IN THE VALLEY
BESETTING SINS

Preparation

Again use the prayer of St. Ignatius of Loyola (see page 85). Reflect on the images or metaphors which St. Ignatius used to describe the life of discipleship: cost, fight, wounds, labor, rest, reward. Is your commitment to doing God's will as strong as that expressed in the prayer? Alternatively, you may want to sing a hymn or recite Psalm 16 or Psalm 47 as your preparation.

Scripture: Read Mark 9:42-50.

Most scholars think that this collection of Jesus' sayings was originally grouped in the early church by the repetition of key words. The verbal phrase *cause to sin* in verses 42, 43, 45, 47 is the linking phrase. The word *fire* in verses 48 and 49 provides the link there. The word *salted* in 49 and 50 connects those three sayings. Probably, these sayings were linked this way to be memorized by catechists. In Mark's hands, however, they serve another function. They provide a very strong warning that discipleship demands a radical rooting out of obstructions and a radical commitment to doing the will of God.

JOURNEY INWARD
Hearing and Seeing

Lent is a time for self-examination and honest self-evaluation. What is there in your life that "causes you to sin"? The ancient fathers spoke of "besetting sins," taking their terminology from Hebrews 12:1, which speaks of "laying aside the sins which . . . beset us" (KJV) (literally, "the sins that stick to us like clothing"). By these they meant those traits within an individual's personality or those habits which were the weak spot in a person's spiritual life. For some it might have been a tendency to sexual lust, for others it might have been gluttony. For some it may have been pride or a critical spirit. Each person had his or her weak point, the point where each was most vulnerable to spiritual attack by evil. What are your "besetting sins"? Writing them in your journal or in the space below may prove a salutary exercise in reality.

What action will you have to take to "cut off" the offending part? Are you beginning to understand that discipleship has a cost?

Meditation and Prayer

After you have reflected on the scripture, enter a period of silence and meditative prayer. Remember to use the centering prayer formulas as you have need of them. After you have become centered, let these words of Jesus become the focal point of your attention:

> Every one who does evil hates the light, and does not come to the light, lest his deeds should be exposed. But he who does what is true comes to the light, that it may be clearly seen that his deeds have been wrought in God.
>
> John 3:20-21

You may want to picture Christ with a searchlight, turning it on your life and lighting up the corners of darkness where the "snakes and toads and monsters" are lurking. Let the light shine in. It will burn away the darkness and whatever lives in it.

Remember that the light of Christ can never hurt you. It can only destroy what is harmful in you. It may feel painful if you have become deeply attached to your besetting sins, but it will be the pain that a surgeon causes while performing a lifesaving operation.

Pray for those persons who you allow to bring out the worst in you, that Christ's light may shine into their lives also.

Conclude with the Lord's Prayer.

JOURNEY OUTWARD

Begin to educate yourself on a significant issue for our society. Some examples are abortion, apartheid, AIDS, homelessness, and hunger. Read, watch documentaries, and talk to people who are knowledgeable on the issue you've chosen. Since this will be an ongoing project, begin today by choosing which issue to focus on. Record any learnings in your journal, such as who is involved, how they are affected, what government is doing about the issue, what the church is doing about it, and whether you are directly or indirectly affected.

JOURNEY TOWARD JERUSALEM
BECOMING ONE

Preparation

Sing or pray this hymn:

> When morning gilds the skies
> My heart awakening cries:
> May Jesus Christ be praised!
> Alike at work and prayer,
> To Jesus I repair:
> May Jesus Christ be praised!

Scripture: Read Mark 10:1-12.

This is one of the more difficult passages in the Gospel. It sounds so rigid and inflexible. But we must be careful not to use it as a proof text to create an absolute prohibition of divorce. In the context of Jesus' controversy with the religious authorities who understood women to be the property of their husbands and therefore as easily disposable as livestock or real estate, Jesus' extreme statement provided a needed safeguard for the sanctity of marriage and the rights of women. The key statement in the scripture reading is the quotation from Genesis which puts the whole question of marriage into perspective as a creation ordinance, designed as the foundation of all human society and relationship.

In a day when marriage has again become cheapened and the vows of marriage held lightly, the strength of this statement is needed. However, we must also guard against making divorce an unpardonable sin. Any broken relationship is an expression of and result of sin, but we must never limit the grace or mercy of God which is capable of transforming even our worst failures.

JOURNEY INWARD
Hearing and Seeing

All of us, whether married or not, enter into interpersonal relationships. Reflect for a few moments on the relationships with others in which you're involved. If you are married, think about your relationship with your spouse. Are you putting the goal of "becoming one" as the highest priority, or are you still trying to hang on to other relationships which interfere with that goal?

If you are unmarried, you may want to think about your friendships and your relationships with family members or neighbors. Are you allowing yourself to be open and transparent in those relationships so that you move from loneliness to intimacy (not sexual intimacy, but the deep sharing of yourself with another)?

Make a list of things (situations, relationships, possessions) that you will need to "leave" in order to "cleave" to your spouse, your friend, or God. Begin to form a plan of action in regard to your list.

Meditation and Prayer

Get into your state of inner quietness before God. Just "be" to God in loving silence.

As you become aware of ways in which you have failed to leave the things or relationships which are preventing you from achieving a deeper level of intimacy with your spouse or someone else, confess these failures to God and begin, in God's presence, to let go of them.

Conclude with the Lord's Prayer.

JOURNEY OUTWARD

The rhythm of personal and corporate prayer continues. Today is the day for remembering you are an important member of the Body of Christ. Join your worship with that of the whole church, past and present, here and around the world. Let today be a sabbath for you. Remember that today is a day to rest from your labors as God rested after Creation. Take a walk outdoors if weather permits, or take a nap in your favorite recliner, or go on a family outing, or read a good detective story, or do whatever else is a way of resting and relaxing for you. The point is to unwind, to let go. Relax and see today as a gift for your renewal and restoration.

JOURNEY TOWARD JERUSALEM
CHILDLIKE INNOCENCE

Preparation

Pray this prayer to begin your time. Since it is short, try to commit it to memory as soon as possible.

Lord, when I awake, and day begins, waken me to thy presence; waken me to thine indwelling; waken me to inward sight of thee, and speech with thee, and strength from thee, that all my earthly walk may waken into song, and my spirit leap up to thee all day, all ways.[11]

Scripture: Read Mark 10:13-16.

These sayings about children and childlikeness may be variations of the same sayings Mark used in 9:33-37. For Mark, at any rate, the image of discipleship as childlikeness is an important one.

JOURNEY INWARD
Hearing and Seeing

What particular qualities of children does Jesus seem to be referring to in verses 14-15? Why are such qualities necessary for entering the kingdom of God?

In what attitudes and areas of your life have you become jaded or overly sophisticated so that you have lost a childlike innocence and simplicity? What will be required of you if you are to regain simplicity, trust, and a holy innocence toward others and toward God?

Meditation and Prayer

Meditate in silence, bringing yourself as fully as you are able into a state of quiet alertness and attentiveness before God. If noises, either inside or outside you, create a distraction, briefly examine each distraction to see if it may be something about which God is trying to get your attention. If so, make it part of your prayer; if not, discard it and, if necessary, use one of the meditation formulas to help you center.

Pray for others as they enter your consciousness. Begin also to make the issue(s) you are studying a matter of prayer. In this way, you are becoming God's agent of reconciliation and healing in the world.

Conclude with the Lord's Prayer.

JOURNEY OUTWARD

Continue to educate yourself about the issue(s) you've chosen. Ask yourself two questions as you study: What is my response to this as a human being? What is my response to this as a Christian?

JOURNEY TOWARD JERUSALEM
PLEDGING ALLEGIANCE

Preparation

Again, pray the prayer introduced yesterday. Reflect on how its petitions give meaning to the Apostle Paul's phrase "Christ in you, the hope of glory" (Col. 1:27).

Scripture: Read Mark 10:16-31.

The amazement of the disciples in verse 24 may be explained by the fact that in the culture of Jesus' day wealth was seen to be a sign of God's blessing upon a person, while poverty was seen, to some extent at least, as a sign of God's disfavor. The exchange between Peter and Jesus about what has been left behind to follow Jesus, particularly the mention of leaving family, probably indicates that within Mark's community were people for whom loyalty to Christ meant divisions and alienation in their families. This passage also connects with the definition in 3:31-35 of what constitutes real family.

JOURNEY INWARD
Hearing and Seeing

The thrust of this story is that attachments to anything or anyone which take precedence over one's attachment to the kingdom of God are obstacles which hinder one from entering the kingdom. The question raised is, What commands my highest allegiance? Ask yourself that question. Like the young man in the story, are you owned by your possessions? What are the things in life which compete for your allegiance and loyalty? To whom do you pledge allegiance—your job? your mortgage? your family? the American flag? your fraternal organization?

When you have analyzed what exerts a claim on your loyalties, then ask yourself what would be involved for you to pledge your *highest* loyalty to the kingdom of God. Do not be content with vague generalities. Allegiance to the kingdom demands action as specific as Jesus' command to the young man. What concrete action, what revisions of priorities, what re-orientation will be demanded of you if you heed Jesus' call to "Go, sell . . . come, follow?"

Meditation and Prayer

When you have prayed for your own needs and those of others which present themselves to your mind, enter into a period of meditative prayer. Do not try to form mental images or words. Simply try to be as present to God as possible and to empty yourself of all distractions or concerns as much as possible. Use a formula if you need to, or look at or "through" a particular object until you become inwardly still and attentive to God. Don't be discouraged if you still have difficulty with wandering thoughts, with inner or outer noises that distract you, or with lack of a feeling of God's presence. Many of the greatest saints constantly struggled with such difficulties. But continual practice will make you more adept at maintaining an inner stillness and alertness. When distractions come, as they will, discard them; or simply return to verbal prayer, perhaps using one of the prayers you've used during the preparation time.

Conclude with the Lord's Prayer.

JOURNEY OUTWARD

Talk with someone else about the issue with which you've chosen to become involved. This person may be your spouse, a friend, your pastor, or a colleague. Let her or him know why you've chosen to focus on that issue, why it concerns you, and that you're trying to find ways to engage the issue out of your Christian faith. Later, record any helpful insights or suggestions that may have come from your sharing.

JOURNEY TOWARD JERUSALEM
TRUE GREATNESS

Preparation

Use the prayer "God Be in My Head" to recollect yourself and become present to God. Perhaps you will also want to sing a hymn or listen to a piece of music which will help you get in the right attitude for prayer.

> God be in my head, and in my understanding;
> God be in mine eyes, and in my looking;
> God be in my mouth, and in my speaking;
> God be in my heart, and in my thinking;
> God be at mine end, and at my departing.

Read Scripture: Mark 10:32-45.

Mark repeats for the third time Jesus' announcement of his Passion to his disciples. As in the earlier two occurrences, the story which follows the announcement illustrates the disciples' failure to grasp what he is saying. Verse 45 might be seen as the climactic point of the entire Gospel; it captures Mark's understanding not only of Jesus but also of what it means to follow him. It could hardly be more forceful than it is, coming as it does after the squabble between James and John over who is the greatest. Pay particular note to the question Jesus asks James and John. That question will figure prominently in the next reading passage as well.

JOURNEY INWARD
Hearing and Seeing

As you open yourself to hear the word of God, let Christ ask you, "What do you want me to do for you?" Spend some time honestly and thoroughly reflecting on your answer. What are the deepest desires of your heart?

Meditation and Prayer

Pray for insight into the meaning of servanthood and how it will become the model for your life. Ask the Lord to lead you to those people and situations whom you are to serve sacrificially. As you become aware of specific persons or situations, note them here or in your journal.

Spend time in silent, contemplative prayer, forming as few mental images as possible.

Conclude your meditative time with the Lord's Prayer.

JOURNEY OUTWARD

Continue to follow whatever issue(s) you've chosen. Begin to formulate a specific plan of action regarding your involvement. Praying about the issue is first and basic. Someone has said that rather than thinking that we can do nothing except pray, we should think that we can do nothing *until* we have prayed. Assuming that the issue(s) is already part of your prayer, where is that prayer leading you in terms of specific involvement?

JOURNEY TOWARD JERUSALEM
REGAINING OUR SIGHT

Preparation

Again use the prayer "God Be in My Head" (see page 95) and spend some time reflecting on and praying each petition. Think of specific ways each petition could be answered in your life. Remind yourself that God does want to fill you as completely as what the prayer asks.

Scripture: Read Mark 10:46-52.

The story of the healing of Blind Bartimaeus is one of the most significant passages in the Gospel of Mark. In fact, it may be seen as the closing bracket around the central part of the Gospel dealing with the meaning of discipleship (the two-stage healing of the blind man in 8:22-26 was the opening bracket). Like the earlier story of the healing of blindness, it serves as both a climax to what has come before and a transition to what follows. Note Mark's skillful literary contrast between Bartimaeus and James and John by his technique of having Jesus ask precisely the same question of the blind man as he asked his ambitious disciples. Also note how the "seeing" imagery functions here. The result of Bartimaeus's regaining his sight is that he "followed [Jesus] on the way"; that is, he became committed to Jesus as a disciple.

JOURNEY INWARD
Hearing and Seeing

Enter into the story imaginatively. Picture yourself as Bartimaeus, sitting along the roadside, blind and unloved. Now Jesus is coming along. You've heard about him (one of the functions of the Gospel to this point has been to tell you about Jesus). Now he's approaching you. You cry out to him. Others try to turn you aside, but you persist. Now Jesus hears your cry and asks you that most important question, the question full of all sorts of possibilities: "What do you want me to do for you?"

How will you answer? Will you ask for something trivial or worldly like James and John did, or will you, like Bartimaeus, ask to regain your sight?

Ask yourself if you have been as persistent in wanting your inner blindness healed as Bartimaeus was to regain his eyesight.

In your case, what will *regaining your sight* mean? Be specific in your reflection. Writing your answer below or in your journal will help you be honest and concrete.

Meditation and Prayer

Spend some time in meditative prayer, perhaps using the cry of Bartimaeus as your centering prayer, "Jesus, Son of David, have mercy on me."

Conclude with the Lord's Prayer.

JOURNEY OUTWARD

Be attentive today to the needs of those closest to you. Concentrate on "seeing" them and making time for them in your day. Perhaps you will want to volunteer to help one of your children or your spouse with a project or with the housework. Cook a family dinner with special care. Call a friend whom you know is lonely or hurting. Do something specific that will let those closest to you know you don't take them for granted but really care for them.

JOURNEY IN JERUSALEM
TRIAL AND PERSECUTION

Preparation

Sing or pray the following hymn:

> Jesus, the very thought of thee
> With sweetness fills the breast;
> But sweeter far thy face to see,
> And in thy presence rest.
>
> O hope of every contrite heart,
> O joy of all the meek,
> To those who fall, how kind thou art!
> How good to those who seek!

Scripture: Read Mark 13:1-23.

The readings for today and tomorrow are slightly out of the order in which Mark arranged his Gospel. However, most scholars agree that chapter 13 stands alone and that Mark has inserted it in its present position. It was not originally part of the Passion narrative, and we want to focus on that narrative during Holy Week. Chapter 13 has many similarities to apocalyptic literature, which was a distinctive literary genre reflecting a particular theological world view within Judaism in the period between the return from exile (*ca.* 520 B.C.) and the end of the first century of the Common Era. Literature of this genre makes use of images of cosmic upheavals which parallel social upheavals on the historical plane. It contains cryptic and even coded references. Hence we see the imagery of darkened suns and falling stars. If you are interested in learning more about apocalyptic literature and thought, you might want to borrow the *Interpreter's Dictionary of the Bible* from your pastor or church library and read the relevant articles.

JOURNEY INWARD
Hearing and Seeing

The imagery of persecution is prevalent here, suggesting that Mark's community was facing such trials of its faith. In verses 3-8, there is a warning against false messiahs who lead people astray. Thinking of the term *messiah* as a deliverer from present difficulties, what are some of the false messiahs you are tempted to follow when you are experiencing a time of testing and trial?

In verses 9-13, there is both the description of persecution and trial which will come to the followers of Jesus, as well as his promise of the courage and wisdom of the Holy Spirit in the midst of trial. What is there in your experience of Christian faith that would be considered so threatening to the world that it would mark you as a target of persecution? What does this tell you about the radical nature of faithful discipleship? Have you ever experienced the kind of power or authority from outside yourself that Jesus talks about in verse 11? If so, describe that experience. If not, try to imagine what situation(s) in your life need such authority.

Meditation and Prayer

In your time of silence, examine your own level of spiritual commitment and faithful discipleship. Allow the Lord to show you lovingly those areas of your life where your level of faith is so shallow that it would hardly merit attention, much less persecution, from the world.

Pray for those Christian brothers and sisters who must endure a great hardship for the sake of Christ, such as those in South Africa who witness against apartheid or those in our own inner cities who struggle against homelessness or the drug traffic.

Conclude your time with the Lord's Prayer.

JOURNEY OUTWARD

If you have chosen to fast on Fridays, today will be a fasting day for you. The length of the fast is at your discretion. Use your fasting time to work on your project for this week—either by further acquainting yourself with the issue(s) you have been studying, or by praying for those concerned, or by engaging in whatever action you have decided upon.

JOURNEY IN JERUSALEM
KEEPING AWAKE

Preparation

Sing or pray this hymn:

> Thou hidden source of calm repose,
> Thou all-sufficient love divine,
> My help and refuge from my foes,
> Secure I am if thou art mine;
> And lo! from sin and grief and shame
> I hide me, Jesus, in thy name.
>
> Jesus, my all in all thou art,
> My rest in toil, my ease in pain,
> The healing of my broken heart,
> In war my peace, in loss my gain,
> My smile beneath the tyrant's frown,
> In shame my glory and my crown.

Scripture: Read Mark 13:24-37.

In this part of chapter 13, the imagery appears to refer less to historical events and more to cosmic events. In verses 24-27, the *parousia,* or second coming, of Christ appears to be imminent. This and other passages in the New Testament have given rise to the opinion among scholars that many people in the earliest Christian communities expected the return of Christ in glory during their lifetime. There is here, however, a strong warning against speculating on the exact time of this hoped-for event, a warning we would do well to heed also.

JOURNEY INWARD
Hearing and Seeing

Without getting into speculation about what the Second Coming would look like, what does the promise of Christ's return mean to you personally? What element, if any, does it add to your faith?

In the closing verses of this chapter, Jesus repeatedly enjoins vigilance upon his disciples: "Take heed, watch . . . Watch therefore . . . what I say to you I say to all: Watch!" What will it mean in your life to exercise this kind of vigilance? Where are you in danger of "falling asleep"?

Meditation and Prayer

Meditate on the "blessed hope" of the Christian—the promise of Christ's return in glory. Pray that this hope may come alive in your life.

Pray also for strength to keep awake and vigilant in those situations where "sleep" (inattentiveness) is a danger for you.

Conclude your time with the Lord's Prayer.

JOURNEY OUTWARD

In regard to the particular issue(s) on which you have been concentrating, where is vigilance demanded as you wait for the coming of the Lord? Reflect on what that coming would mean for that particular issue or situation. How does it change your perspective on it or on your involvement with it? Does it seem to indicate one action rather than another?

DAY 40

PALM SUNDAY

JOURNEY IN JERUSALEM
TRIUMPH BEFORE TRAGEDY

Preparation

Today is the beginning of Holy Week. As much as possible, try to live the events of this week with Jesus. This week is the climax not only of the events in Jesus' life or of the Gospel of Mark, though it certainly is both of these. It is also the climax of this journey in the spiritual life that you have been taking in company with others. The prayer which will be used in the preparation time all this week reflects the climactic nature of the week. Today, simply read over the whole of the prayer from John Wesley's Covenant Service, both the part the minister says and the part the people say. Reflect on the radical nature of the petitions and the cost to you of entering into such a covenant with God.

The Minister:

And now, beloved, let us bind ourselves with willing bonds to our covenant God, and take the yoke of Christ upon us.

This taking of his yoke upon us means that we are heartily content that he appoint us our place and work, and that he alone be our reward.

Christ has many services to be done; some are easy, others are difficult; some bring honor, others bring reproach; some are suitable to our natural inclinations, and temporal interests, others are contrary to both. In some we may please Christ and please ourselves; in others we cannot please Christ except by denying ourselves. Yet the power to do all these things is assuredly given us in Christ, who strengthens us.

Therefore let us make the covenant of God our own. Let us engage our heart to the Lord, and resolve in his strength never to go back.

Being thus prepared, let us now, in sincere dependence on his grace and trusting in his promises, yield ourselves anew to him. . . .

The People:

I am no longer my own, but thine. Put me to what thou wilt, rank me with whom thou wilt; put me to doing, put me to suffering; let me be employed for thee or laid aside for thee, exalted for thee or brought low for thee; let me be full, let me be empty; let me have all things, let me have nothing; I freely and heartily yield all things to thy pleasure and disposal.

And now, O glorious and blessed God, Father, Son, and Holy Spirit, thou art mine, and I am thine. So be it. And the covenant which I have made on earth, let it be ratified in heaven. Amen.

Scripture: Read Mark 11:1-11, 15-19.

The Palm Sunday story is a familiar one—almost too familiar. We think we know it well, but do we really? For one thing, the text doesn't tell us that the general population of Jerusalem welcomed Jesus into the city as we normally envision; it tells us that those who had accompanied him there hailed him as a king coming to reclaim the throne of David. Also, there is little evidence in the text to explain why a huge crowd who would hail him as the heir of David one day would turn on him and crucify him a few days later. The immediate cause of Jesus' arrest and trial is cloaked in mystery. It is difficult to tell from the Gospel narratives what Jesus did that could have provoked a sentence of crucifixion from the Romans, a fate normally reserved for revolutionaries or others who posed threats to the state.

JOURNEY INWARD
Hearing and Seeing

Imagine yourself as one of those who followed Jesus to Jerusalem. Your shouts of "Hosanna" welcoming "the kingdom of our father David" betray your continued misunderstanding of what Jesus is about. As far as we know, Jesus himself never claimed the title Son of David—a royal messianic title. Was the kingdom of God, which formed the content of Jesus' preaching and teaching, only a return to the political and nationalistic glory of King David's reign? Or was it something more? What this text forces us to do is to ask, Who is Jesus for me? What do I expect to get out of this journey I've been on with him? Am I expecting Jesus to solve all my problems? Do I want uninterrupted inner tranquility? Do I want a narcissistic kind of self-awareness and self-knowledge? What are my expectations? Reflect on these questions in the space below.

Jesus' action in driving out the businessmen from the Temple was a shocking act. What might be a comparable act of Jesus in your life? Where are the "money-changers" which have taken over the temple? What would it mean for Jesus to say to you, "You have taken what was meant to be a 'house of prayer for all the nations' and turned it into a 'den of robbers'?"

Since today is Sunday, a day to join in the corporate prayer of the church, take this reflection a step further. What in your church would Jesus want to drive out were he to come in today? What will it mean for your congregation or parish to "become a house of prayer for all the nations"?

Meditation and Prayer

In your prayer time, open yourself up for Christ to come and cleanse your inner temple. Let the Holy Spirit show you all the dark corners, the pockets of corruption or pride or unresolved conflicts which prevent you from being a clean vessel.

Conclude your time with the Lord's Prayer.

JOURNEY OUTWARD

Join your personal prayers with the corporate prayer of the people of God. Remember that prayer is not private; even when we pray as individuals, we are never alone. We are always in the company of saints. So make that reality visible today by being present at the corporate service of worship.

Also, let today be a sabbath for you. Accept the day as a divine gift of time for remembering God and for renewal of yourself through relaxation and rest. Unwind, let go, relax! Since God intends us to live life in a sabbath rhythm of work and rest, there's no need to feel guilty about deliberately resting from our labors.

JOURNEY IN JERUSALEM
STEWARDS OF THE VINEYARD

Preparation

Today, reflect on just the first part of the Covenant Prayer, the part assigned to the minister (see Day Forty, page 104). Pay particular attention to the way the "yoke of Christ" is defined. Think about what a yoke is and its purpose. Remind yourself of how privileged you are that Christ should want to yoke himself to you!

Scripture: Read Mark 11:27–12:12.

The question of Jesus' authority is brought to a sharp point of focus in the incident of the cleansing of the Temple. This sets the context for the questions from the chief priests and scribes about Jesus' authority and also the context for the parable of the tenants in the vineyard, which follows.

JOURNEY INWARD
Hearing and Seeing

Imagine your own life as the vineyard. What kind of fruit is the Master expecting of you? Are you holding yourself accountable as a steward of God's vineyard, your life? What kind of fruit are you producing? For whose benefit?

Whose authority do you answer to? Why?

Meditation and Prayer

Spend some time in meditative prayer. Let your spirit go out in love, embracing God in love where you cannot embrace God in understanding.

While in an attitude of love for God, imagine that love stretching wide enough to include others in it, both friends and enemies or those from whom you are estranged.

Conclude your time with the Lord's Prayer.

JOURNEY OUTWARD

Since this is Passion week, begin to look around you and determine the point at which you can identify most keenly with the sufferings of Christ. The emphasis here is not on what someone else is suffering or doing to identify with Christ's sufferings but on what around you will become the cross for you. It may be a certain relationship in which you're involved. It may be a difficult or painful experience you're going through. It may be a particular issue of social injustice which affects you. What within that situation can make it a means of identifying with the sufferings of Jesus?

JOURNEY IN JERUSALEM
PUTTING GOD FIRST

Preparation

Again reflect on the first part of the Covenant Prayer of John Wesley (see Day Forty, page 104). Let the requirements of discipleship call you to humility and poverty of spirit as you approach God.

Scripture: Read Mark 12:13-17, 28-34.

These are examples of controversy stories, which were common in the Gospel tradition. They show Jesus in controversy with his opponents and emphasize his superior spiritual authority. The question in focus in both these stories is: What are our obligations, and to whom do we owe them?

JOURNEY INWARD
Hearing and Seeing

Taking Jesus' statement "Render to Caesar the things that are Caesar's and to God the things that are God's," begin to reflect on those two realms of authority as they exert claims on your life. If Caesar represents the authority of the State, as in this story, how does that authority impinge on your life and lay claim to it? Jesus appears to be saying that Caesar (the State) has certain legitimate claims and that God has certain legitimate claims. The implication is that these will sometimes conflict, demanding decision as to one's primary allegiance. In what ways in your own experience do the claims of the state conflict or compete with the claims of God? Whose authority is primary? In other words, is Caesar's authority derived from the greater authority of God, or is it an authority which is itself ultimate?

The second story amplifies the first. How does the first commandment illuminate the question of whose authority must be primary in our lives? Can you begin to see how an answer that God's authority has highest claim might lead to suffering at the hands of Caesar? Where is the point of focus of that conflict between God and Caesar in your life? How far are you from the kingdom?

Meditation and Prayer

You might want to make a list below or in your journal of the areas of your life where you see these two realms of authority making claims. Head one column "Caesar" and the other column "God." When you have made your lists, see if there are areas of actual or potential conflict.

Pray for courage to put God's claims first. Conclude with the Lord's Prayer; then spend some moments reflecting on this prayer which you have been saying every day. Are you beginning to better understand its richness and its radical nature?

JOURNEY OUTWARD

Think about the issue(s) you focused on last week in terms of this Caesar/God dualism. Does this way of conceiving it help you in deciding what specific action you need to be taking? If you haven't yet done something specific with regard to that issue, begin today.

JOURNEY IN JERUSALEM
DOING A BEAUTIFUL THING

Preparation

Read over the part assigned to the people in the Covenant Prayer (see Day Forty, page 104). Do not pray this prayer simply as a matter of course. It calls for too much to be treated in a cavalier way. Let the first phrase which underlies all the other petitions begin to sink into your consciousness: *I am no longer my own, but thine.* Does that phrase fill you with joy or with dread?

Scripture: Read Mark 12:41-44; 14:1-11.

In Mark's Gospel, women are often the most devoted followers of Jesus. Though these two stories have no formal connection, reading them together helps to illuminate Mark's answer to the question, What does it mean to follow Jesus?

JOURNEY INWARD
Hearing and Seeing

Ask yourself, *Am I giving to God out of my abundance, or am I giving all I have?* Let this question apply not only to your possessions but to your whole self.

By the title of his book about her, Malcolm Muggeridge has characterized the work of Mother Teresa among the dying in Calcutta as *Something Beautiful for God*. What "beautiful thing" are you doing for Christ? What extravagant commitment of yourself are you making, what costly perfume are you spreading around for no motive other than sheer love for Jesus?

Meditation and Prayer

Read these stories a second time. As you do so, enter into them imaginatively and let them become part of your prayer. Become the women in the stories as you sit in God's presence. Make an offering of your life.

Conclude with the Lord's Prayer.

JOURNEY OUTWARD

Be on the lookout for something beautiful you can do for God or for a situation in which you can give your "whole living" and thus render some service to Christ. Perhaps visiting with a shut-in, volunteering to help in a meal program for the homeless, or writing a letter to a friend you've been out of touch with could be your act of beauty. Don't just think beautiful thoughts. *Do something!*

MAUNDY THURSDAY

JOURNEY IN JERUSALEM
IN THE UPPER ROOM AND GETHSEMANE

Preparation

If you feel you can do so with a whole heart, pray the Covenant Prayer (see page 104). Don't worry about whether or not you might fail at some point. Of course you will, as we all do. What is important is your intent. Can you, with all that you are right now, all that makes up your selfhood at this moment, say these words and mean them?

Scripture: Read Mark 14:12-72.

Though Mark's own hand is not quite as evident in the Passion narrative as in other parts of his Gospel, he did shape this material significantly. In the story of the Last Supper, Jesus predicts his disciples' desertion. When Mark relates the story of Jesus' arrest, he shows the accuracy of that prediction with a dramatic sentence, "They all forsook him and fled." Except for the even more cowardly betrayal by Peter, that is the last we hear of the disciples in this Gospel! In addition, Mark adds a brief account of a young man, clad only in a linen cloth, who literally jumps out of his clothes to get away. Though some have speculated that this is Mark himself making a cameo appearance, the theory is highly unlikely. What is more likely is that there is some connection, mysterious to us, between the young man in verse 51 and the young man who greets the women at the empty tomb in chapter 16. The same word is used for both, and both are said to be clothed in a linen garment.

JOURNEY INWARD
Hearing and Seeing

Let these familiar stories penetrate your mind and heart with new power. Read them with imagination by entering into the story yourself and being one of the participants.

Are you Judas, eating with Jesus in fellowship one moment and betraying him the next? We are all Judas at some time. As you become aware of your Judas nature, bring it to the Lord in confession, seeking forgiveness and healing.

Are you Peter, boasting of your commitment and undying loyalty one moment and denying that you ever knew Jesus when the heat's turned on? At some time or other, we are all Peter, too. Bring this part of your nature to the Lord in confession, seeking forgiveness and healing.

Are you among the other disciples of whom it is said (verse 50), "And they all forsook him and fled"? The disciples don't fare too well in these stories. Theirs is "exemplary disbelief." Perhaps there's hope for us with our denials and betrayals and flights from reality. Confess your own brokenness and fear.

Enter into Jesus' agony and decision in Gethsemane. Where is your own Gethsemane? What is the situation, the issue, the cross which faces you and which you desperately want to avoid? Can you say, "Not what I will, but what thou wilt"?

Meditation and Prayer

As a way of praying on this solemn day, you may wish to use one of the Maundy Thursday hymns, such as "Go to Dark Gethsemane" or "'Tis Midnight and on Olive's Brow," to help you enter imaginatively into our Lord's Passion. Pray for others you know who are going through a dark night of suffering or confusion.

Conclude with the Lord's Prayer.

JOURNEY OUTWARD

If there is someone who has been hurt by your faithless behavior, find that person and seek to be reconciled. If there is a situation where you are struggling with self-will versus God's will, share that struggle with someone as a means of helping you come to a decision to follow God's will.

(If your prayer and meditation time is during the afternoon or evening hours, look ahead to the "Meditation and Prayer" and the "JOURNEY OUTWARD" sections for tomorrow, Good Friday.)

GOOD FRIDAY

JOURNEY IN JERUSALEM
THE ROAD TO THE CROSS

Preparation

Read or sing this hymn by Charles Wesley as you prepare to observe this solemn day.

> O Love divine, what hast thou done!
> The immortal God has died for me!
> The Father's co-eternal Son
> Bore all my sins upon the tree.
> Th' immortal God for me hath died:
> My Lord, my Love is crucified!
>
> Is crucified for me and you,
> To bring us rebels back to God.
> Believe, believe the record true,
> You all are bought with Jesus' blood.
> Pardon for all flows from his side:
> My Lord, my Love is crucified!
>
> Behold him, all ye that pass by,
> The bleeding Prince of life and peace!
> Come, sinner, see your Savior die,
> And say, "Was ever grief like his?"
> Come, feel with me his blood applied:
> My Lord, my Love is crucified!

Scripture: Read Mark 15:1-39.

Mark gives the centurion's awe-filled statement in verse 39 special force by linking it with the sight of Jesus' dying moment. Here the "seeing" imagery reaches a climax that sums up Mark's message. "When the centurion . . . *saw* how he died, he said, 'Truly this man was the Son of God!'" (AT) This is the answer to the question Mark raised in 4:41: Who is this man? It is significant that it is answered not by one of the disciples but by a Roman soldier, a pagan who has just overseen Jesus' execution. What Mark is saying is, If you really want to see the Son of God, this is where you have to look. This is where you get the second touch that brings clear sight. You don't look at miracles, at signs and wonders. You look at the cross. The cross tells you who Jesus really is.

This clear sight, however, can only be gained when one looks at the cross in faith and in the commitment to be a disciple. For Mark, seeing and following are inextricably linked.

JOURNEY INWARD
Hearing and Seeing

Jesus is on the cross. Our rebellion, our self-enthronement, our desire to be God put him there. And each time we give in to self-will, to self-centered ways of living, we drive the nails deeper; we "crucify" the Son of God afresh and "put him to an open shame" (Heb. 6:6, KJV). In your mind, place yourself in the crowd around the cross of Jesus. Let the reality of the consequences of human sin—your sin—be driven home to you.

What are the sins in your life which form the thorns in his crown or the nails in his hands?

Meditation and Prayer

You may find it deeply meaningful to spend the hours between noon and 3:00 P.M. in silence and in meditation if circumstances permit. Or, perhaps you will be able to attend a three-hour Good Friday service. By giving this extended time to meditate on the meaning of Jesus' death for us, you will greatly enrich your observance. You might find it helpful to structure your three-hour time of meditation around the words of Jesus on the cross. You would need to look at the crucifixion story in all the Gospels to include all seven "words."

The cross is not only the symbol of death but also the symbol of life, for on it Jesus bore the destruction that our sins and our self-centered lives should have brought upon us. So as you wait at the cross today, mourn the sins that put him there but also "feel his blood applied," as Charles Wesley so aptly put it. Let today truly become *Good* Friday for you.

Conclude with the Lord's Prayer.

JOURNEY OUTWARD

If you have elected to fast from food on Fridays, continue to do so. You might also want to fast from speech during the three hours from noon until 3:00 P.M.

Attend services at your church or wherever Good Friday services are being held in your community. This is a day when we need to engage in corporate prayer and confession as well as individual prayer. We need to journey to the cross with all God's people. To fully appreciate the joy of the Easter celebration, it is necessary to spend Good Friday at the foot of the cross.

JOURNEY ENDED
FOR THE TIME BEING

Preparation

After yesterday's meditation on the crucifixion of Jesus, can you pray the Covenant Prayer (see Day Forty, page 104) with more depth of will and intent today?

Scripture: Read Mark 15:40-47.

Again, the women are the heroes in Mark's eyes. They are the ones who stick by Jesus through thick and thin. The story of the burial was preserved by the church to guard against charges by opponents that Jesus' death had been faked, as well as to guard against heretical doctrines such as Docetism (the belief that Jesus only appeared to have a physical body and therefore only appeared to die a real death). The Apostles' Creed also affirms Jesus' death—"was crucified, dead, and buried."

JOURNEY INWARD
Hearing and Seeing

Meditate on the fact that when Jesus was buried, our sins (and therefore our own deaths) were buried with him. The church has always viewed baptism as a re-enactment of our burial with Christ. The Apostle Paul wrote,

> Do you not know that all of us who have been baptized into Christ Jesus were baptized into his death? We were buried therefore with him by baptism into death, so that as Christ was raised from the dead by the glory of the Father, we too might walk in newness of life. For if we have been united with him in a death like his, we shall certainly be united with him in a resurrection like his. We know that our old self was crucified with him so that the sinful body might be destroyed and we might no longer be enslaved to sin. For he who has died is freed from sin.
>
> Romans 6:3-7

What are the sins in your life that you have not yet consciously buried with Christ?

Meditation and Prayer

Charles Wesley, in his hymn "O For a Thousand Tongues to Sing," has a liberating line: "He breaks the power of canceled sin, he sets the prisoner free." The sin was canceled on the cross. Not only is the debt of sin canceled but the power of the sin that has already been canceled is broken. Are you still carrying a load of guilt from sin that has already been canceled? If so, it is time to realize that when Jesus was buried, you were buried with him—your old self with all its sin is gone. You are a new creation in Christ. You are free! Rejoice and give thanks for that freedom.

Conclude with the Lord's Prayer.

JOURNEY OUTWARD

Are you the agent through whom someone else is still under the power of canceled sin? In other words, are you applying guilt or using other persons' guilt as a means of control or manipulation? If you are, release those persons. Go to them and freely and honestly forgive them and let them know they are forgiven.

THE DAY OF RESURRECTION

JOURNEY BEGUN AGAIN
BACK TO GALILEE

Preparation

Sing! Sing anything that makes you happy! Today is not a day for introspection but a day for celebration. So celebrate!

Scripture: Read Mark 16:1-8.

Did Mark intend his Gospel to end at verse 8, or has the original ending been lost? The other endings you may have in your translation (everything after verse 8) are almost universally recognized to be later additions because various scribes couldn't conceive of Mark wanting to end the Gospel at verse 8. I'm convinced that Mark could very well have intended to end the Gospel there, or rather, begin the Gospel again at verse 8; for the ending sends the women (and the readers) back to the beginning—to Galilee. Here is the last occurrence of the seeing imagery also. "He is going . . . to Galilee; there you will *see* him." In other words: Continue on the journey. Make a new start. This time you will see clearly. Having followed Jesus to the cross, you will now journey with the Risen Christ, who has the power to open blind eyes.

JOURNEY INWARD
Hearing and Seeing

In your imagination, put yourself in the place of those women at the tomb. Can you feel something of their amazement at hearing the announcement "He is risen, he is not here"?

If, as the Apostle Paul says, Christ's resurrection means that we now walk in "newness of life" (Rom. 6:4), what shape will that newness take in your life? Use your journal or the space provided to reflect on this. What old patterns of thought or behavior in your life have been buried with Christ? What new patterns of thought or behavior are now to take their place?

As you hear the command to go to Galilee, what will you be looking for this time? What will continuing this journey mean for you? This is a good time to reflect on where you have been, how you have come to the place in your journey where you now are, and where you are going from here. Easter is not the end of the journey but a new beginning. (Use the next page to record your reflections.)

Let your prayer time today be one of praise and celebration. Let the reality of God's aliveness begin to sink into your consciousness. As you read and reread the Gospel of Mark, let Christ's living presence come to you through the stories there.

Conclude with the Lord's Prayer.

JOURNEY OUTWARD

Look around you for evidence (it may only be *seen* with eyes of faith) that Christ is alive, that God has conquered the powers of death, and that there is hope not only for us as individuals but for the whole world. Share the good news with someone.

Happy journeying!

SUGGESTIONS FOR GROUP USE

Although *A Lenten Journey* was designed for individual use, it may also be used in a group setting. The suggestions below may facilitate its use by a group in a local church during Lent.

1. Plan for a weekly meeting of those using the book. A Sunday evening meeting might prove to be the best time, since the structure of the book tends to build toward the Sundays of Lent, each of which is a "little Easter." But any day or evening will work. The main consideration is regularity.

2. Give out the manual the Sunday before Ash Wednesday. At this initial meeting, introduce the book not only as an individualized approach to developing a deeper spiritual life but also as a tool for building relationships within the Body of Christ. At this initial meeting, involve the group in some community-building sharing. The following questions may be useful as discussion starters:

   a. Why have you signed up to participate in this Lenten journey? What has been going on in your life that has made you feel a need for a deeper life of prayer and relationship with God?

   b. What are some of the struggles you've been having with growing in your life with God? What do you find difficult about prayer?

   c. What's the most important thing you are hoping for as you begin this journey in the spiritual life?

   You might want to close the group time with a period of silence or with conversational prayer where members may pray short sentence prayers as they are led. You could also sing a chorus or say the Lord's Prayer together.

3. A plan for the weekly meetings during Lent might proceed in the following manner (though each group should feel free to develop the style of interaction that is most meaningful for its members):

   a. Sit in a circle facing each other or around a table. Begin with a hymn or some choruses. If someone can play the guitar or piano, so much the better.

   b. To start the sharing, focus on what was the most meaningful daily exercise that week, especially in the "Journey Inward" sections of the exercises. Don't force anyone to talk, but encourage each person to share which of the daily exercises meant the most to her/him and why.

   c. After everyone who wishes has had a chance to share what was most meaningful or important, ask about the concept, idea, or insight which seemed most difficult to understand or put into practice. Try to avoid negativism at this point. The idea is not to put down anyone else's experience but to share honestly one's own struggles in a loving and caring setting.

   d. Next, share any interesting or significant experiences arising out of the "Journey Outward" sections, along with insights into how these experiences are related to one's inner life.

e. Since prayer is corporate as well as personal, spend some time praying together. If you are an experienced group pray-er, be careful not to dominate this time. Encourage open sharing of needs for which the others may pray in love. You might want to vary the time from week to week between silent intercession and vocalized prayers. Or you might want to practice some group meditational prayer with everyone using one of the prayer formulas or mantras introduced in the exercises, saying them silently or softly while doing deep rhythmical breathing. Close your time together with song or with the Lord's Prayer or with a benediction which all say together.

NOTES

1. A. W. Tozer, *Born after Midnight* (Harrisburg, PA: Christian Publications, 1959).

2. Richard J. Foster, *Celebration of Discipline* (San Francisco: Harper & Row, 1978), 1.

3. The Myers-Briggs Type Indicator is a helpful tool for self-discovery, particularly for becoming aware of the manner in which one's personality prefers to function. One resource which attempts to correlate personality type with preferred forms of prayer or spirituality is *Prayer and Temperament,* by Chester P. Michael and Marie C. Norrisey (Charlottesville, VA: The Open Door, Inc., 1984).

4. Abraham Joshua Heschel, *Quest For God* (New York: Crossroads, 1982), 10.

5. Ronald Klug, *How to Keep a Spiritual Journal* (Nashville: Thomas Nelson Publishers, 1982), 17–26.

6. Henri J. M. Nouwen, *The Way of the Heart* (New York: The Seabury Press, 1981), 25–26.

7. David Fleming, *Modern Spiritual Exercises* (Garden City, NJ: Image Books, 1983), 14.

8. Abba Isaac's *Second Conference on Prayer,* cited in Basil Pennington, *Centering Prayer,* (Garden City, NY: Image Books, 1982), 28.

9. I am indebted for this insight to Dr. Robert Traina, formerly professor of English Bible at Asbury Theological Seminary.

10. John Wesley, *Journal,* vol. 1 (London: The Epworth Press, 1938), 472–476.

11. *Acts of Devotion,* ed. George Appleton (London: SPCK, 1966), 63.

BIBLIOGRAPHY

Appleton, George, ed. *Acts of Devotion*. London: SPCK, 1963.

Fleming, David. *Modern Spiritual Exercises*. Garden City, NY: Image Books, 1983.

Foster, Richard J. *Celebration of Discipline*. San Francisco: Harper and Row, 1978.

Heitzenrater, Richard P. *The Elusive Mr. Wesley,* Vol. 1. Nashville: Abingdon, 1984.

Heschel, Abraham Joshua. *Quest For God*. Crossroads: New York, 1982.

Klug, Ronald. *How to Keep a Spiritual Journal*. Nashville: Thomas Nelson Publishers, 1983.

Nouwen, Henri J. M. *The Way of the Heart*. New York: Seabury Press, 1981.

Pennington, M. Basil. *Centering Prayer*. Garden City, NY: Image Books, 1982.

Tozer, A. W. *Born After Midnight*. Christian Publications: Harrisburg, PA, 1959.

Wesley, John. *Journal,* vol. 1, London: The Epworth Press, 1938.

ABOUT THE AUTHOR

Larry R. Kalajainen is pastor of the United Methodist Church at New Brunswick in New Jersey. He and his wife served six years as World Division missionaries in Sarawak, East Malaysia. During this time he developed a strong interest in spiritual formation and has read widely among ancient spiritual masters as well as modern spiritual guides.

Mr. Kalajainen holds the B.A. degree from the University of Pittsburgh, the M.Div. from Asbury Theological Seminary, the Th.M. in New Testament from Princeton Theological Seminary, and the M.Phil. from Drew University Graduate School, where he is currently a Ph.D. candidate in New Testament Studies. He is a member of the Society of Biblical Literature and considers himself a "teaching pastor." He serves as adjunct professor in the Division of Contemporary Ministries at Drew Theological School.

An avid photographer, Mr. Kalajainen concentrates on fine-art photography for gallery exhibitions.

He is married to Carol, a teacher of English-as-a-Second Language. They have two daughters, Kristin and Katherine.